COSTUME 1066-1966

JOHN PEACOCK

COSTUME 1066-1966

THAMES AND HUDSON

To Paul Hernon, with grateful thanks
for help and encouragement

Calligraphy by Rachel Yallop

First published in the United States in 1986 by
Thames and Hudson Inc., 500 Fifth Avenue,
New York, New York 10110
Reprinted 1988

Library of Congress Catalog Card Number 85–51950

Printed and bound in Great Britain by
Richard Clay Ltd, Chichester, Sussex

Contents

Preface

The aim of this book is to present a systematic documentation of the changes in costume of both men and women since 1066. I have used the reigns of the kings and queens of England as a framework, and have selected examples which represent the main changes in each period, which best show the continuing development of costume style, and which reflect similar trends in continental Europe. The order within each reign is also chronological.

It is not my intention to present an academic history, nor do I claim this to be an exhaustive survey of every costume of every period. The sketch-book approach I have adopted, with brief explanatory notes, is designed to make any costume self-explanatory, and will enable the reader to trace the evolution of a particular style or garment, from its conception to its full blossoming, its exaggeration and its inevitable demise. Where a particular garment undergoes significant changes, I have devoted a special section to it (see pp. 13, 19, 21).

Fashion has always been created by the wealthier classes and not, until recently, by the man in the street. The costumes which I have illustrated are therefore those which in general have been worn by rich people, and by civilians rather than any particular group such as the military or the Church.

Between the early Middle Ages and the sixteenth century, costume evolved very slowly but, as can be seen from the illustrations, changes occur with increasing frequency after that, until by the end of the eighteenth century fashion as we understand it today – with its denigration of the unfashionable – was born. Fashion became something to be followed closely by men and women of position, with attention paid to the time of year, the hour of the day, town or country, the occasion, and the various degrees of formality or informality. Fashion etiquette became a strict discipline, reaching its height in the late nineteenth and early twentieth centuries, and lasting until comparatively recent times.

The most improbable ideas have been adopted by those dedicated to being fashionable – the long pointed shoes and towering headdresses of the fifteenth century, the beribboned petticoat breeches and cascading wigs of Charles II's court, the huge hats and restrictive hobble skirts worn by the Suffragettes of all people, and the winkle-picker shoes of the 1950s, their ancestry traceable from the reign of Edward II – all of them absurd but all of them worn in perfect seriousness.

The subject of fashion in costume presents a wide field for research, and published information is increasingly available to the modern student. The list of Further Reading on p. 127 gives the main reference books I have used in the preparation of this sketch book, with brief descriptions of each.

John Peacock

WILLIAM I · 1066~87

short cropped hair

round neck

low round neck

short sleeves with embroidered borders

longer hair

cord belt

twisted fabric belt

leather belt

sleeves to elbow

simple undergown

embroidered, painted or woven patterns

side split

long fabric trousers

long trousers bound with leather to knee

leather shoes

leather shoes

soft leather shoes

veils held by leather, fabric or metal bands

'V'shaped necklines

round neck with centre opening

long flared sleeves

short sleeves

cord belt with tassels

embroidered borders

short gown

dark undergown

brightly coloured and patterned fabrics

soft leather slippers

embroidered hemline

7

WILLIAM II · 1087~1100

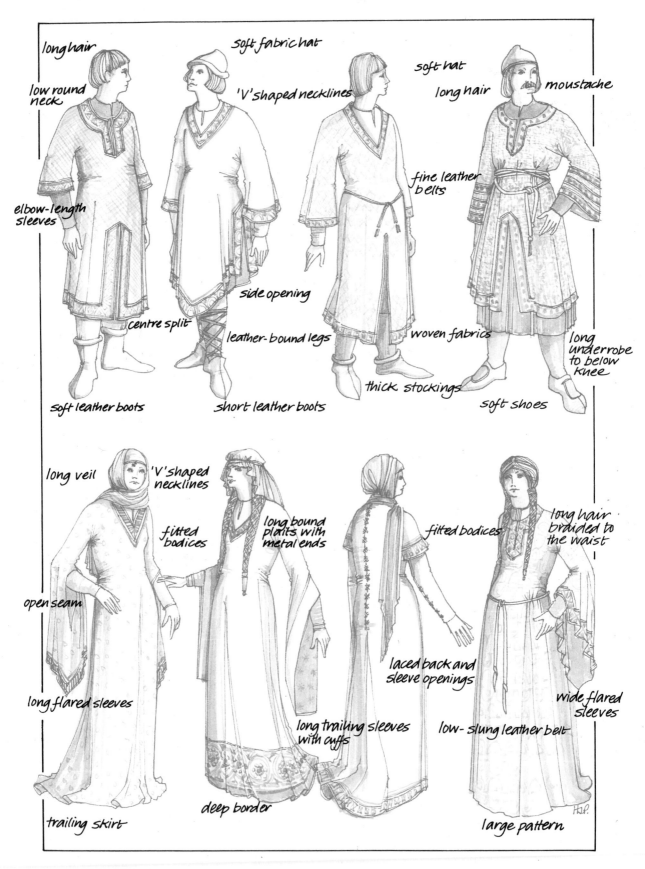

long hair

low round neck

elbow-length sleeves

soft leather boots

centre split

soft fabric hat

'V' shaped necklines

side opening

leather-bound legs

short leather boots

soft hat

long hair

moustache

fine leather belts

woven fabrics

thick stockings

long underrobe to below knee

soft shoes

long veil

'V' shaped necklines

fitted bodices

long bound plaits with metal ends

open seam

long flared sleeves

trailing skirt

deep border

long trailing sleeves with cuffs

laced back and sleeve openings

fitted bodices

long hair braided to the waist

wide flared sleeves

low-slung leather belt

large pattern

HENRY I · 1100~35

long fringed hair

beard

moustache

shoulder-length hair

beards and moustaches

turn-back cuff

low belt

long sleeves

double leather belt

centre opening

sleeves more flared

side opening

long patterned undergown

deep embroidered hem and sleeve

two-tier skirts

embroidered leather shoes

soft-leather shoes

long veil

long plaited hair

laced side openings

fitted bodices

tightly fitted bodices

decorative painted leather belt

patterned linings

trailing sleeves

wide trailing sleeves

knotted sleeves

trailing hems

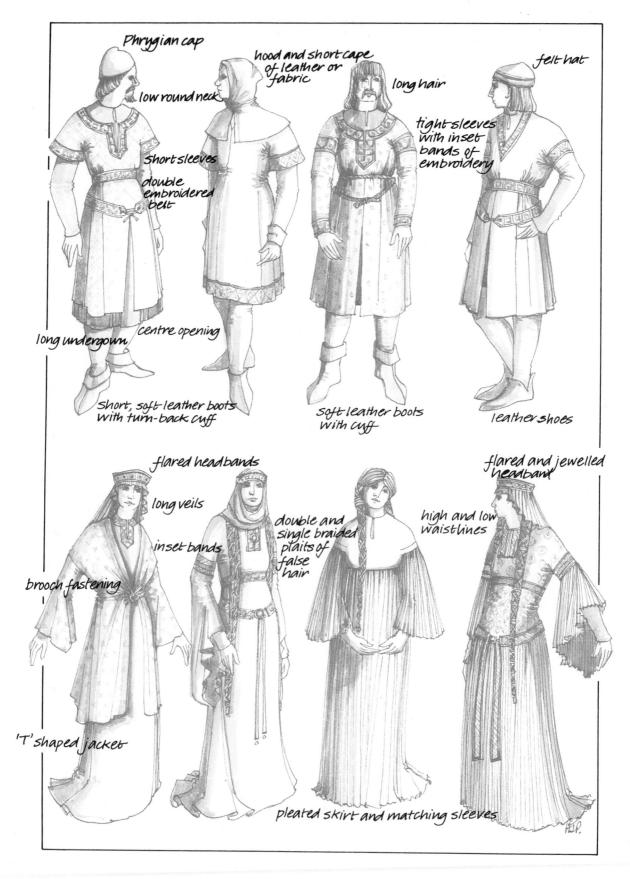

Phrygian cap

hood and short cape of leather or fabric

felt hat

low round neck

long hair

tight sleeves with inset bands of embroidery

short sleeves

double embroidered belt

long undergown

centre opening

Short, soft leather boots with turn-back cuff

soft leather boots with cuff

leather shoes

flared headbands

flared and jewelled headband

long veils

double and single braided plaits of false hair

high and low waistlines

inset bands

brooch fastening

'T' shaped jacket

pleated skirt and matching sleeves

HENRY II · 1154–89

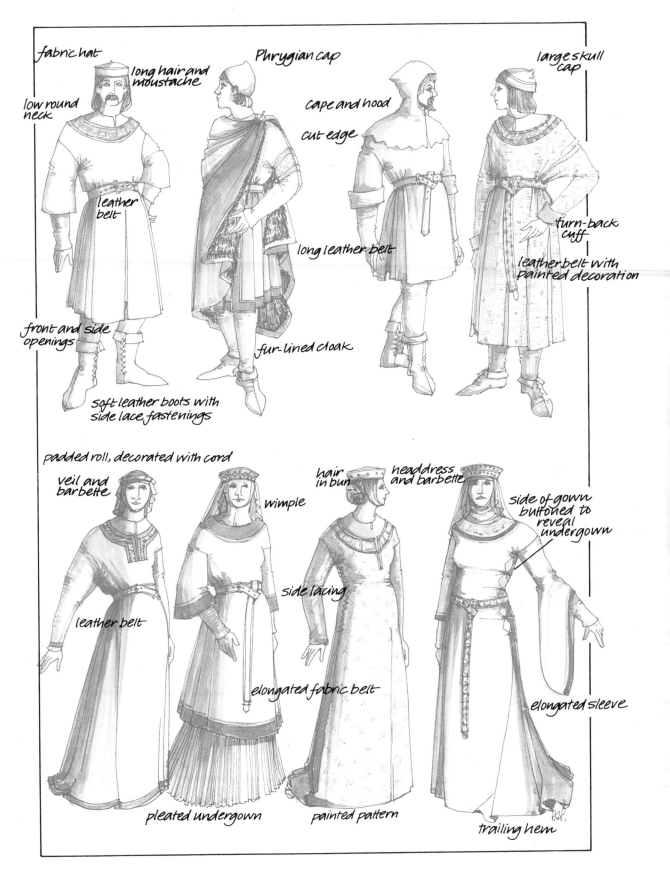

fabric hat

long hair and moustache

Phrygian cap

large skull cap

low round neck

cape and hood

cut edge

leather belt

long leather belt

turn-back cuff

leather belt with painted decoration

front and side openings

fur-lined cloak

soft leather boots with side lace fastenings

padded roll, decorated with cord

veil and barbette

wimple

hair in bun

headdress and barbette

side of gown buttoned to reveal undergown

leather belt

side lacing

elongated fabric belt

elongated sleeve

pleated undergown

painted pattern

trailing hem

RICHARD I · 1189~99

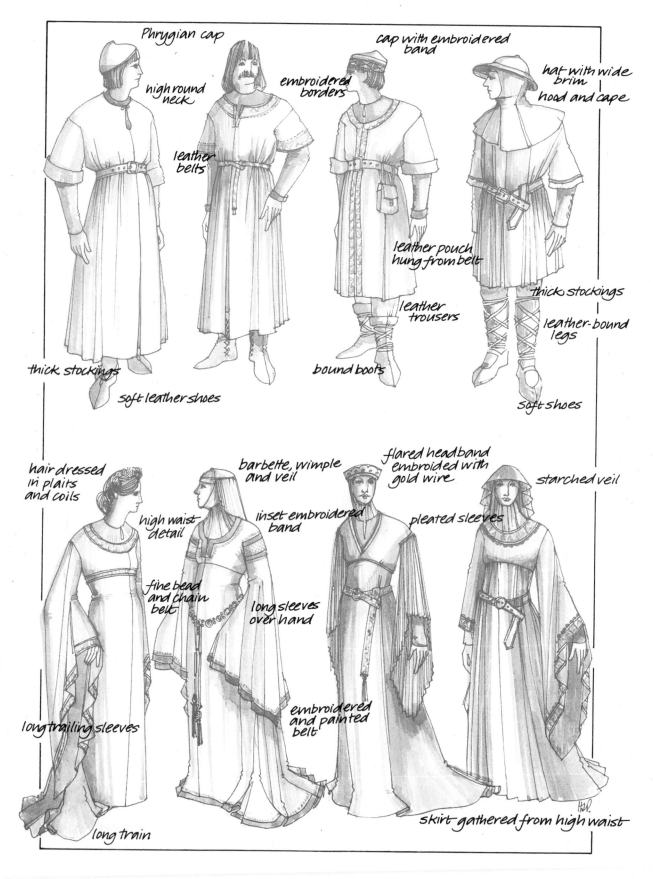

Phrygian cap

cap with embroidered band

high round neck

embroidered borders

hat with wide brim
hood and cape

leather belts

leather pouch hung from belt

thick stockings

leather trousers

leather-bound legs

thick stockings

bound boots

soft shoes

soft leather shoes

hair dressed in plaits and coils

barbette, wimple and veil

flared headband embroided with gold wire

starched veil

high waist detail

inset embroidered band

pleated sleeves

fine bead and chain belt

long sleeves over hand

long trailing sleeves

embroidered and painted belt

long train

skirt gathered from high waist

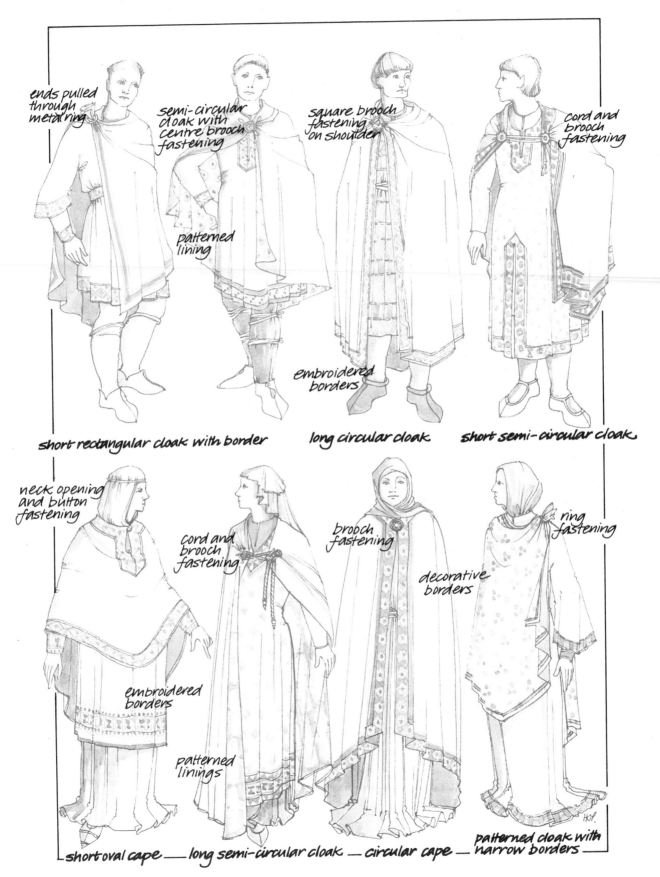

ends pulled through metal ring

semi-circular cloak with centre brooch fastening

square brooch fastening on shoulder

cord and brooch fastening

patterned lining

embroidered borders

short rectangular cloak with border

long circular cloak

short semi-circular cloak

neck opening and button fastening

cord and brooch fastening

brooch fastening

ring fastening

decorative borders

embroidered borders

patterned linings

short oval cape — **long semi-circular cloak** — **circular cape** — **patterned cloak with narrow borders**

13

JOHN · 1199~1216

ring and pin brooch

soft felt hat with braid decoration

cape with hood

dagged edge

hats with stalks and cut, turn-back brims

inset embroidered bands

embroidered cuffs

folded leather belt

embroidered gauntlets

soft leather bag

leather bindings

skirt cut into panels

thick hose

ankle straps

flat leather shoes

long boots with cuffs and pointed toes

flat, embroidered cap over veil and barbette

deep embroidered circlets

long veils

crenellated circlet over veil and wimple

ring and pin brooch

set-in sleeves

long ruched undersleeve

high waist detail

double belt

low-slung belt

wide cuffs

soft leather purse

softly pleated skirt

wide embroidered hem

trailing hem

14

HENRY III · 1216 ~72

soft cap over a coif

laced-in sleeve

buttons

embroidered gauntlets

dagged hemline

long leather boots

embroidered cap

undertunic sleeve

striped tunic

hanging oversleeve

split skirt panels

soft footwear

buttons

cape and hood with dagged edge

button fastening

painted leather shoes and boots

coif

hood

gathers and pleats

opening slit at waist level

gauntlets

wide sleeves to knee

supertunic (overcoat)

crispinette

laced-in, contrast fabric sleeves

side lacing

barbette worn over hat

buttons

sleeveless gowns

open side lacing

gowns worn without a belt or girdle

centre split

high, wide hat with overveil, barbette and wimple

overgown with open side

soft girdle

train

fur hat worn over coif

button fastenings

long point on hood

lirapipe (very long point on hood)

button fastening

pleated sleeve head

buttons

dagged edges

deep armhole

split sleeve

dagged hem

open sides

thick hose

patterned hose

soft roll-down shoes

short boots

more pointed toes

long hide boots

hat with draped wimple

circlet over crispinette

hat, crispinette and scalloped barbette

circlet and veil over draped wimple

overgowns draped from neckline

deep armholes

undergown sleeves

sides caught with lacing

button fastening

patterned fabrics

applied bands of contrast fabric

short overtunic with embroidered hem

H.R.

hood with lirapipe

button fastenings

hood with lirapipe to hem, over overtunic

small hat with shallow brim

lirapipe wound around the head

dagged edge

split in overgown sleeve

leather hip bags

open-sided overtunic with dagged edges

parti-coloured hose

supertunic with decorated sleeves

leather pouch

very short skirt

long wool stockings

soft boots with button fastening

pointed toes

shoes with very long points

hair dressed in rolls

high, wide headdress

crispinette

barbette

large hood

veil

button fastening

securing band

open sides to hipline

tight undersleeves

large patterns

decorated slit openings

open sides to below hipline

cloak

small train

very long train

large pattern

beaver hat with brim

hats worn over hoods

small hat with wide up-turned brim

shoulder cape with hood

button fastenings

shoulder capes with dagged edges

slim-fitting jackets, woven or embroidered

arm bands with streamers

metal hip belts

plain hose

parti-coloured hose

woven or embroidered patterns

parti-coloured hose

dagged tippets

short boots

hose with leather soles

very long points

small hat over barbette

hair plaited over the ears, with veil and wimple

small hat over crispinette and barbette

crispinette hung from a narrow fillet

overgown with open sides

gown buttoned through to hip

fur bodice

use of more than one fabric and pattern

buttons to elbow

slits

long trailing skirts, front and back

CLOAKS AND MANTLES · 1327–77

hood with dagged edge

lirapipe

shoulder fastening

button fastening

dagged hem

short boots

fine metal fillet

elaborately dagged edges

Leather-soled hose

hood arranged to form a hat

hood

buttons to hip

long overtunic

shoulder fastening

extended points

elaborately dagged hem

crispinette and fillet

fur trim

cord fastenings

shaped cloak

ruffled cap and veil

printed and knotted tippet

decorated border

fur-trimmed hems

crispinette and filet

plaited hair

patterned sleeves

ruffled cap

fur overcape

RICHARD II · 1377~99

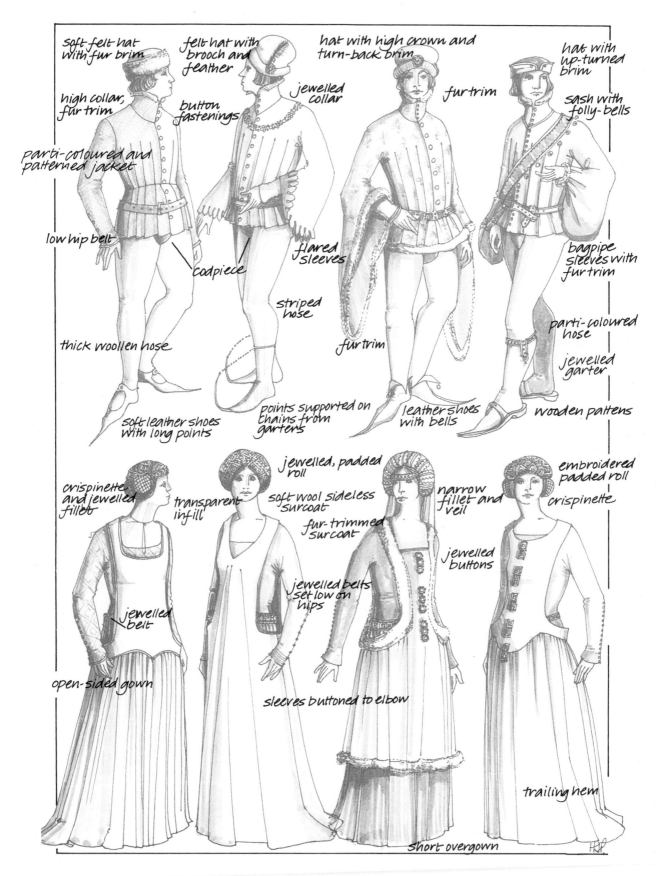

soft felt hat with fur brim

felt hat with brooch and feather

hat with high crown and turn-back brim

hat with up-turned brim

high collar, fur trim

button fastenings

jewelled collar

fur trim

sash with folly-bells

parti-coloured and patterned jacket

low hip belt

codpiece

flared sleeves

bagpipe sleeves with fur trim

thick woollen hose

striped hose

fur trim

parti-coloured hose

jewelled garter

soft leather shoes with long points

points supported on chains from garters

leather shoes with bells

wooden pattens

crispinette and jewelled fillet

transparent infill

jewelled, padded roll

soft wool sideless surcoat

fur-trimmed surcoat

narrow fillet and veil

embroidered padded roll

crispinette

jewelled buttons

jewelled belts set low on hips

jewelled belt

open-sided gown

sleeves buttoned to elbow

trailing hem

short overgown

HOUPPELANDS · 1377~99

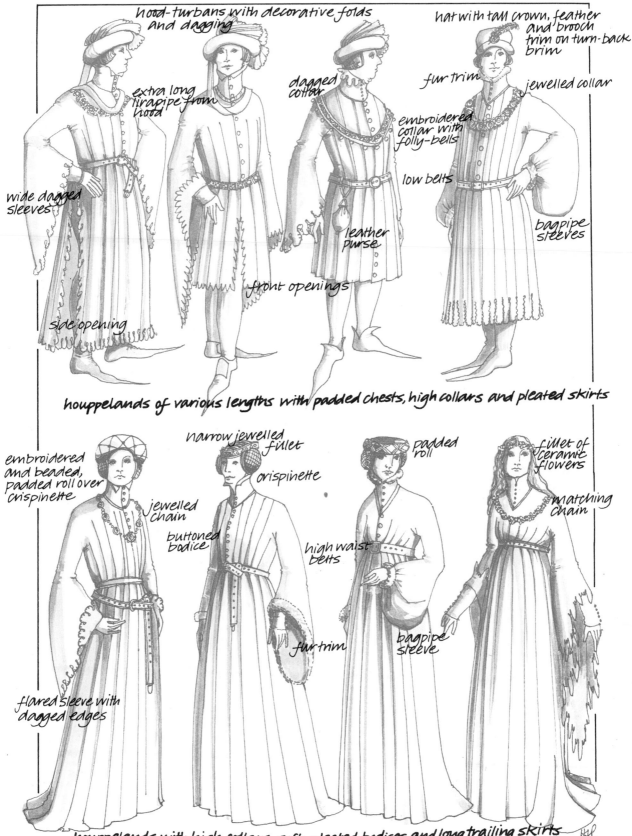

hood-turbans with decorative folds and dagging

hat with tall crown, feather and brooch trim on turn-back brim

extra long liripipe from hood

dagged collar

fur trim

jewelled collar

embroidered collar with folly-bells

low belts

wide dagged sleeves

bagpipe sleeves

leather purse

front openings

side opening

houppelands of various lengths with padded chests, high collars and pleated skirts

embroidered and beaded, padded roll over crispinette

narrow jewelled fillet

padded roll

fillet of ceramic flowers

crispinette

jewelled chain

matching chain

buttoned bodice

high waist belts

flared sleeve with dagged edges

fur trim

bagpipe sleeve

houppelands with high collars, soft, pleated bodices and long trailing skirts

HENRY IV · 1399~1413

padded rolls with dagged decoration

soft high-crowned hat

long decorative lirapipe

high stand collars

jewelled collar

brooch decoration

wide shoulders

padded shoulders

embroidered sash with folly-bells

patterned fabrics

leather belts

leather bag

turn-back cuffs with dagged edges

long dagged sleeves

dark bagpipe undersleeves

dagged hem

fur-trimmed hem and sleeves

patterned lining

soft boots

flat-heeled boots with less exaggerated points

open-sided houppeland

hair worn above the ears under a crispinette

wide padded roll and short veil

large padded crispinette and veil

wide decorated band

padded roll and veil

high stand collars

jewelled collar

button fastenings

embroidered collar and folly-bells

heavy necklace

leather belt with buckle

embroidered belt

high waistlines

embroidered belt with folly-bells

flared sleeves with fur trim

trailing sleeves with dagged edges

bagpipe sleeves

patterned fabric

trailing skirts, front and back

Soft padded roll covered with cut leaf shapes

high stand collar

long dagged sleeves

hose with leather soles

padded roll, soft draped crown

brooch

fur collar and trim

bodice tucked from yoke

leather belt

low hip belt

knee-length tunic

fur-trimmed hem

leather boots

short, curled hair

high stand collars

padded chests

codpiece

patterned fabrics

trailing sleeves

fine leather shoes, shorter points

short hair

fur trim

fur trim

parti-coloured hose with leather soles

embroidered padded roll

flat collar

tucked bodice

heavy necklace

high waist belt

long trailing sleeves

brooch and feather trim

soft padded rolls with cut leaf shapes

embroidered yoke

folly bells

shorter overskirt

fur trim

up-turned collar

embroidered belt

very long trailing sleeves

beaded and embroidered roll

crispinette

short veil

sash and folly-bells

fur trim

full skirt with long train

HENRY V · 1413-22

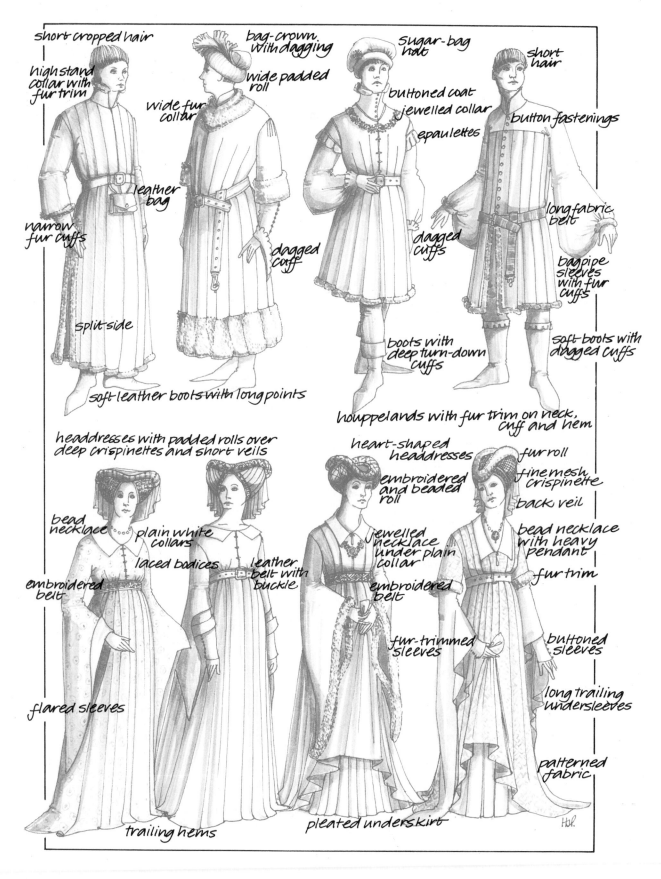

short cropped hair

high stand collar with fur trim

wide fur collar

narrow fur cuffs

leather bag

split side

soft leather boots with long points

bag-crown with dagging

wide padded roll

dagged cuff

sugar-bag hat

buttoned coat

jewelled collar

epaulettes

dagged cuffs

boots with deep turn-down cuffs

short hair

button fastenings

long fabric belt

bagpipe sleeves with fur cuffs

soft boots with dagged cuffs

houppelands with fur trim on neck, cuff and hem

headdresses with padded rolls over deep crispinettes and short veils

bead necklace

plain white collars

laced bodices

embroidered belt

leather belt with buckle

flared sleeves

trailing hems

heart-shaped headdresses

embroidered and beaded roll

jewelled necklace under plain collar

embroidered belt

fur-trimmed sleeves

pleated underskirt

fur roll

fine mesh crispinette

back veil

bead necklace with heavy pendant

fur trim

buttoned sleeves

long trailing undersleeves

patterned fabric

Hol.

short hair

high stand collar with fur trim

laced fastening

split sleeves

fur-trimmed hem and cuffs

wide bagpipe sleeves

codpiece

thick hose

ankle boots with long points

sugar-bag hat

brooch trim

button fastening

slit used as armhole

buttoned undersleeves

scalloped skirt

ankle boots with narrow cuffs and long cuffs

draped padded roll

jewelled collar

embroidered undersleeve

pleated skirt

hose with leather soles

soft sugar-bag hat on padded roll

brooch

brocade fabric

fur trim

open-sided tabard worn over short tunic

dagged cuffs

heart-shaped headdress

high waist belt with brooch trim

dagged edges

horned headdress with dagged veil

bead necklace

long trailing sleeves

wing collars

high waist detail

long sleeves over hands

heart-shaped headdresses

roll covered with petals

short veil

heavy necklace with large stones

fur trim

dagged edges

felt hat with padded brim

soft crown, padded roll

dagged crown

felt hat with soft up-turned brim and brooch trim

gathered sleeves

stand collars

padded roll with draped covering

doublets with stand collar and buttoned front

gathered sleeve

padded fronts

slashed at elbow

fur trim

turn-down cuff

patterned velvet

heavy velvet with stamped pattern

painted and stamped fabrics

fur-trimmed hem lines

long overgowns with front openings

shoes with elongated points

padded roll over headdress

wide headdress with soft veil

high padded roll over tall headdress

headdress with draped and dagged veil

fur collar

fur trim

low 'V' shaped neckline

chin strap

heavy necklace

high waistlines

laced bodice

fur trim

flared sleeve to wrist

long trailing sleeves

embroidered borders

patterned velvets and silks

wide fur-trimmed sleeves and hemline

long trains

undergowns in plain colours

uneven hemline

tall felt hat

fur trim

hat with up-turned fur brim

elaborate chain

pleats

wide fur trim

Knee-length coats

woollen or cotton hose

shoes with long points

short cropped hair

yokes

patterned velvets

short boots

soft draped crown

brooch decoration

fur trim

gathered sleeves

open side

slight train

fur roll over mesh headdress

gathers

low necklines

undergown

high waistline

fur trim

skirts gathered at the front

train

patterned silk

mesh headdress with transparent veil

gathered sleeves

fur cuff

shoulder-length veil

laced underbodice

dress of heavy wool

heart-shaped headdress

wide neckline

large fur hat with hourglass crown

wide brim

short cropped hair above the ears

soft fur hat

felt hat with wide, padded fur roll

padded rolls of fur

high yoke

low 'V' shaped neckline

cartridge pleats

short, full sleeves

tabard belted at the waist

striped bindings

open-sided tabards

sides open to underarm

knee-length boots with turn-down cuffs

wooden pattens

shaded fur trim, matching sleeves and neckline

heart-shaped headdress with long back veil

embroidered headdresses

veils over fine wire frames

embroidery and fine beads

wide, low scooped neckline

heavy necklace

short transparent veils

fine embroidery

fur collar

fine gathers

low 'V' shaped back, fur trim

tight sleeves

high waistlines

fur cuffs

fur trim at wrist

flared cuffs

hemline with plain binding

fur-trimmed hemline

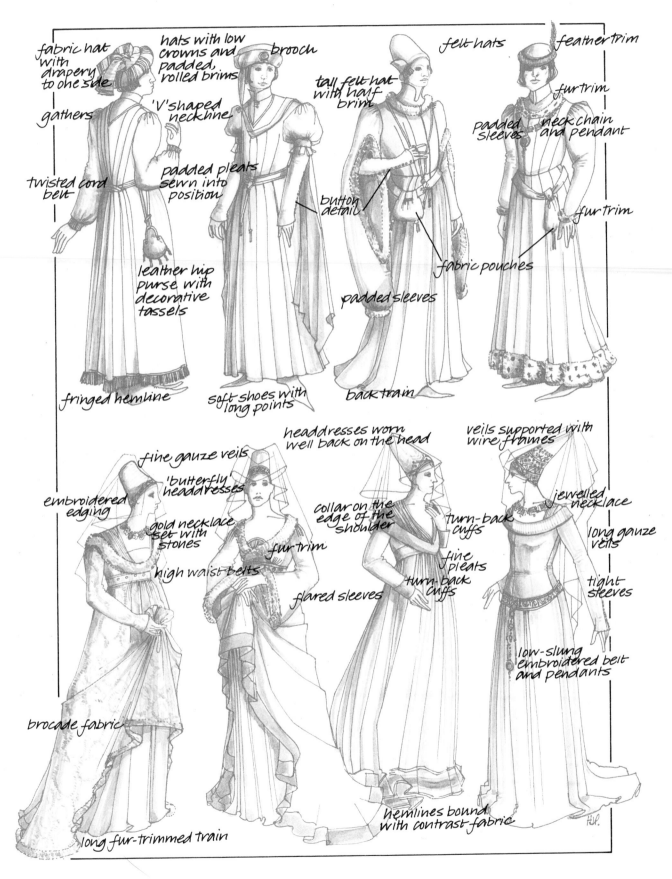

fabric hat with drapery to one side

hats with low crowns and padded, rolled brims

brooch

felt hats

feather trim

gathers

'V' shaped neckline

tall felt hat with half brim

fur trim

padded sleeves

neck chain and pendant

twisted cord belt

padded pleats sewn into position

button detail

fur trim

leather hip purse with decorative tassels

fabric pouches

padded sleeves

fringed hemline

soft shoes with long points

back train

fine gauze veils

headdresses worn well back on the head

veils supported with wire frames

'butterfly' headdresses

embroidered edging

gold necklace set with stones

fur trim

collar on the edge of the shoulder

turn-back cuffs

jewelled necklace

high waist belts

flared sleeves

fine pleats

long gauze veils

turn-back cuffs

tight sleeves

brocade fabric

low-slung embroidered belt and pendants

long fur-trimmed train

hemlines bound with contrast fabric

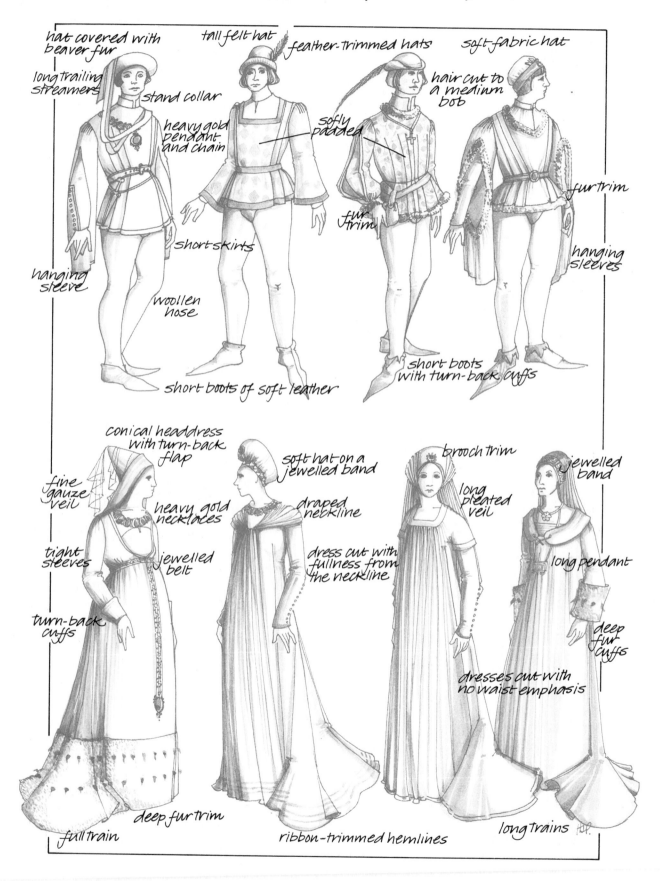

hat covered with beaver fur

tall felt hat

feather-trimmed hats

soft fabric hat

long trailing streamers

stand collar

heavy gold pendant and chain

softly padded

hair cut to a medium bob

fur trim

hanging sleeve

short skirts

fur trim

hanging sleeves

woollen hose

short boots with turn-back cuffs

short boots of soft leather

conical headdress with turn-back flap

soft hat on a jewelled band

brooch trim

jewelled band

fine gauze veil

heavy gold necklaces

draped neckline

long pleated veil

tight sleeves

jewelled belt

dress cut with fullness from the neckline

long pendant

turn-back cuffs

deep fur cuffs

dresses cut with no waist emphasis

deep fur trim

full train

ribbon-trimmed hemlines

long trains

felt hat with double fur roll

soft felt hat

feather trim

small felt hat with rolled brim

beaver hat with brooch trim

high stand collars

neck chain

fur collar

high stiff collar

button detail

gathered sleeves

formal pleats

tight waists

tight undersleeves

very short skirts

fur trim

flared skirts

knotted hanging sleeves

open sleeves

fur-trimmed hanging sleeves

wool or cotton hose worn with a soft gusset

boots with decorative flaps and long points

ankle-length soft leather boots

simple felt hat with binding

tall, stiff headdress with turn-back brim

soft caps with stiff, turn-back brims

brooch trim

undercap

necklace of gold and pearls

heavy gold jewellery

jewelled collar

fur collar

fur collar

brooch trim

high waist emphasis

natural waist position

piped waist seam

turn-back cuffs

very tight sleeves cut long over the hands

belt with chain and purse

contrast fabric hem

ribbon trim

long trains

pleated underskirt

H.P.

soft, low-crowned hats

up-turned brim with cut edge

up-turned brim

brooch

bobbed hair

cutaway brim

fur collar

heavy, jewelled collars

fur trim

wide fur collar

pendant and chain

slashed sleeves

short skirts

deep cuff

laced sleeve

hanging sleeves

long coat with fur lining

leather gaiters

leather shoes with strap

soft leather shoes

tall headdresses worn tilted well back on the head

gold mesh

tall headdress, turn-back brim

fine veil

veil tied under the chin

gold and silver embroidery

jewelled necklace

fur trim

fine gauze veil

necklace and pendant

necklace and pendant

fitted bodice

fitted bodice

embroidery

low belts

laced opening

tight sleeves

fur trim

buttons

buttons

bound hemlines

long trains

HENRY VII · 1485~1509

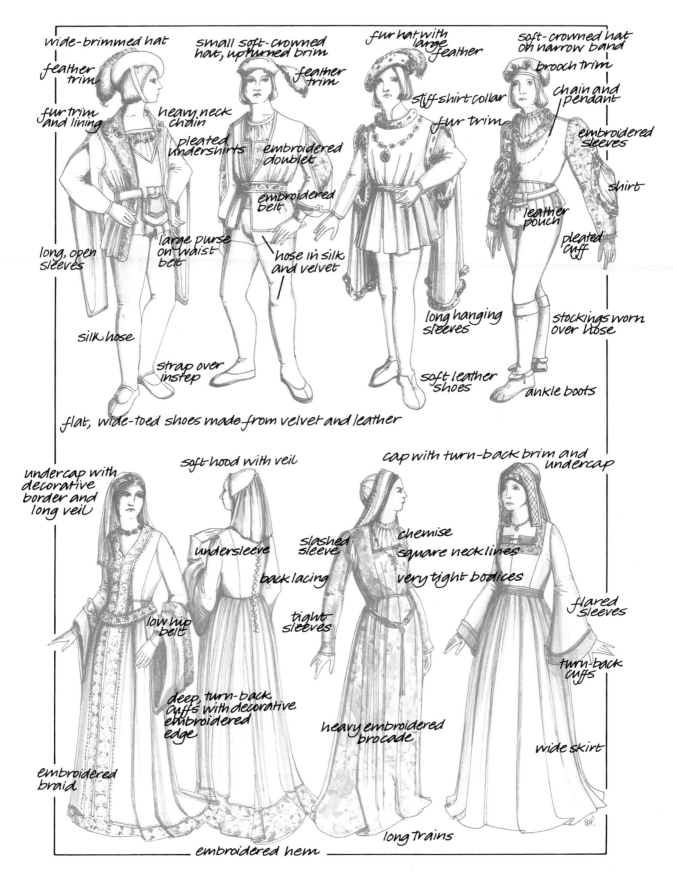

wide-brimmed hat

feather trim

fur trim and lining

long, open sleeves

silk hose

strap over instep

small soft-crowned hat, upturned brim

heavy neck chain

feather trim

pleated undershirts

embroidered doublet

embroidered belt

large purse on waist belt

hose in silk and velvet

fur hat with large feather

stiff shirt collar

fur trim

long hanging sleeves

soft leather shoes

soft-crowned hat on narrow band

brooch trim

chain and pendant

embroidered sleeves

shirt

leather pouch

pleated cuff

stockings worn over hose

ankle boots

flat, wide-toed shoes made from velvet and leather

undercap with decorative border and long veil

soft hood with veil

undersleeve

back lacing

low hip belt

deep, turn-back cuffs with decorative embroidered edge

embroidered braid

cap with turn-back brim and undercap

slashed sleeve

chemise

square necklines

very tight bodices

tight sleeves

heavy embroidered brocade

flared sleeves

turn-back cuffs

wide skirt

long trains

embroidered hem

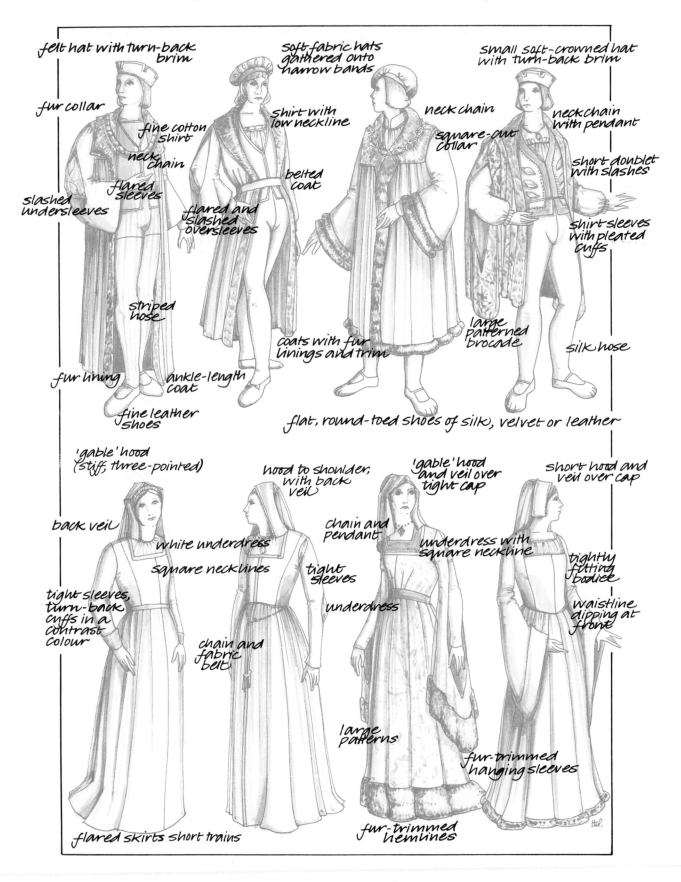

felt hat with turn-back brim

fur collar

fine cotton shirt

neck chain

flared sleeves

slashed undersleeves

striped hose

fur lining

ankle-length coat

fine leather shoes

soft fabric hats gathered onto narrow bands

shirt with low neckline

flared and slashed oversleeves

belted coat

coats with fur linings and trim

neck chain

square-cut collar

large patterned brocade

small soft-crowned hat with turn-back brim

neck chain with pendant

short doublet with slashes

shirt-sleeves with pleated cuffs

silk hose

flat, round-toed shoes of silk, velvet or leather

'gable' hood (stiff, three-pointed)

back veil

white underdress

square necklines

tight sleeves, turn-back cuffs in a contrast colour

hood to shoulder, with back veil

chain and fabric belt

tight sleeves

underdress

'gable' hood and veil over tight cap

chain and pendant

underdress with square neckline

large patterns

short hood and veil over cap

tightly fitting bodice

waistline dipping at front

fur-trimmed hanging sleeves

flared skirts short trains

fur-trimmed hemlines

fur hat

fur collar

shirt

chain and pendant

flared sleeves with fur trim

fabric hose

velvet hat with narrow, turn-back brim

brooch

short bobbed hair

large fur collar

doublet with pleated skirt

fur-trimmed sleeves and hem

padded roll

shirt with stand collar

woollen doublet with large pattern

leather or fabric purses on narrow belts

feather and brooch trim on velvet hat

undershirt

lacing

undershirt

slashed oversleeve

flat, wide, round-toed shoes of fabric or leather, with straps over insteps

cap with brim to the shoulder and back veil

metal necklace of chains and flowers

flared sleeves with wide cuffs

inset panels of braid

undercap, 'gable' hood and veil

square necklines

very tight bodices

open centre panel reveals underdress

turn-back cuffs, lined and trimmed with fur

velvet dress with soft pleated skirt

chain necklace and pendant

square neckline with fur trim

hemlines with deep fur trim

wide 'gable' hood

fine veil

long chain and pendant

stiffened cuffs

patterned velvet

fabric purse on chain belt

35

HENRY VIII · 1509~47

soft fabric crown

flat brim

shirt tied at neck

full puffed sleeves

feather and brooch trim

shirts with high stand collars

up-turned brims

beards and moustaches

hat with silk-taffeta crown and stiff, flat brim

pleated edge to shirt collars

ostrich plume

embroidered sleeves

slashed decoration

separate skirt or base

leather or velvet gloves

decorated codpiece

coats trimmed and lined with fur

slashed sleeves

embroidered gauntlets

short, full and pleated coats of wool, velvet, silk and damask

hose of fine wool or silk

slashed decoration

shoes of soft leather with square-shaped toes

square-toed shoes made from velvet, silk or fine leather

'gable' hood and back veil

hood set back to show hair

French hood and veil

finely pleated linen

'gable' hood with veil

Contrast fabric to fill in square neckline

low square necklines

tight upper sleeves

necklaces of gold and pearls

laced front bodice

back veil to the shoulders

back lacing

soft linen pleating

low, square neckline

tightly fitting bodice

deep cuff, lined with fur

undersleeve of embroidered fabric with slashed decoration

slashed undersleeves

tight sleeves with fur cuffs

frill of fine lining

fine cord girdles

embroidered hanging girdle

richly woven damask

overskirt split to show undergown of contrasting fabric

slight train

36

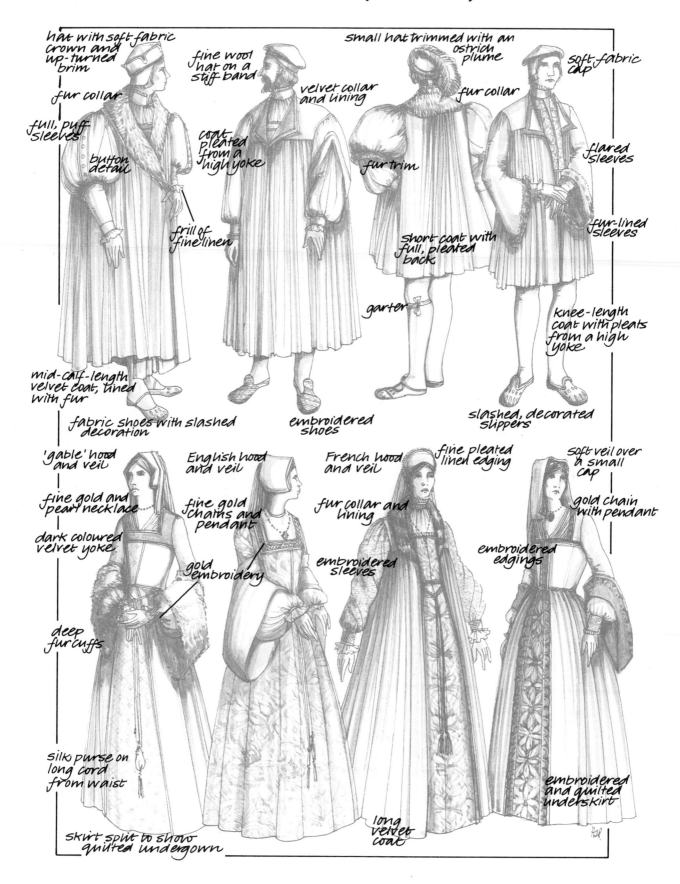

hat with soft fabric crown and up-turned brim

fine wool hat on a stiff band

small hat trimmed with an ostrich plume

soft fabric cap

fur collar

velvet collar and lining

fur collar

full, puff sleeves

button detail

coat pleated from a high yoke

flared sleeves

fur trim

fur-lined sleeves

frill of fine linen

short coat with full, pleated back

knee-length coat with pleats from a high yoke

garter

mid-calf-length velvet coat, lined with fur

fabric shoes with slashed decoration

embroidered shoes

slashed, decorated slippers

'gable' hood and veil

English hood and veil

French hood and veil

fine pleated linen edging

soft veil over a small cap

fine gold and pearl necklace

fine gold chains and pendant

fur collar and lining

gold chain with pendant

dark coloured velvet yoke

gold embroidery

embroidered sleeves

embroidered edgings

deep fur cuffs

silk purse on long cord from waist

embroidered and quilted underskirt

skirt split to show quilted undergown

long velvet coat

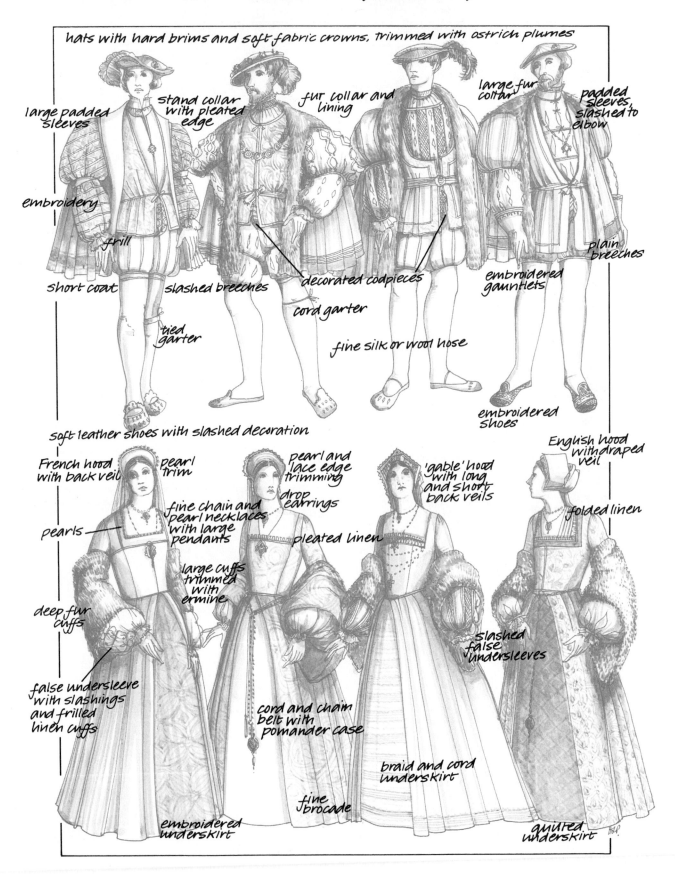

hats with hard brims and soft fabric crowns, trimmed with ostrich plumes

stand collar with pleated edge

fur collar and lining

large fur collar

padded sleeves, slashed to elbow

large padded sleeves

embroidery

frill

short coat

slashed breeches

tied garter

decorated codpieces

cord garter

fine silk or wool hose

embroidered gauntlets

plain breeches

embroidered shoes

soft leather shoes with slashed decoration

French hood with back veil

pearl trim

pearl and lace edge trimming

'gable' hood with long and short back veils

English hood with draped veil

pearls

fine chain and pearl necklaces with large pendants

drop earrings

folded linen

pleated linen

large cuffs trimmed with ermine

deep fur cuffs

false undersleeve with slashings and frilled linen cuffs

cord and chain belt with pomander case

slashed false undersleeves

braid and cord underskirt

fine brocade

embroidered underskirt

quilted underskirt

hats with stiff up-turned brims

feather trim

pearl trim

fabric-covered brim, feather trim

linen frill

slashed decoration showing undershirt

large padded sleeve

high stand collar with narrow linen frill

neck chains

deep fur collar and lining

fur trim

slashed sleeve decoration

decorated codpiece

embroidered gauntlets

chain- and cord-belted coat

plain breeches

full, pleated coat

velvet band edged with gold braids

full, fur-lined coats with broad shoulders and large padded and slashed sleeves

flat shoes with slashed decoration

embroidered shoes

English hood with pad and back veil

pleated linen headdress with veil

French hood with fine pearl edging and back veil

linen frill

pleated linen

button trim

wing collar

filled-in neckline

square neckline with pearl edging

chains and pendants of gold and pearls

slashed sleeve tied with gold cords

false undersleeve with cuff and frill

split, laced bodice

twisted gold belt with long tassel

pomander case on chain belt

heavy brocade with embroidery

brocade with gold re-embroidery

embroidered and quilted underskirt

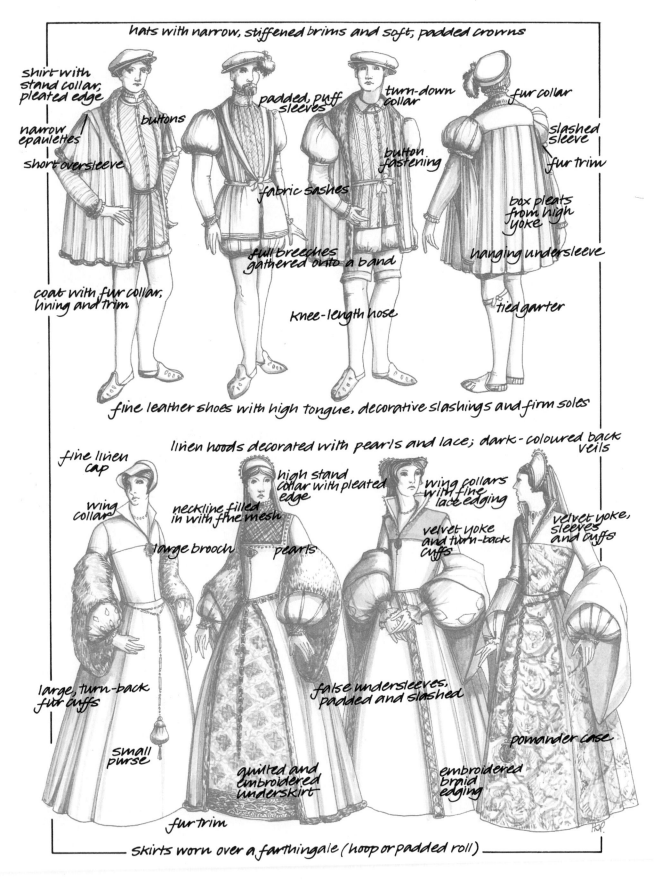

hats with narrow, stiffened brims and soft, padded crowns

shirt with stand collar, pleated edge

narrow epaulettes

short oversleeve

buttons

padded, puff sleeves

turn-down collar

fur collar

slashed sleeve

fur trim

button fastening

fabric sashes

box pleats from high yoke

hanging undersleeve

full breeches gathered onto a band

coat with fur collar, lining and trim

knee-length hose

tied garter

fine leather shoes with high tongue, decorative slashings and firm soles

linen hoods decorated with pearls and lace; dark-coloured back veils

fine linen cap

wing collar

high stand collar with pleated edge

wing collars with fine lace edging

velvet yoke, sleeves and cuffs

neckline filled in with fine mesh

velvet yoke and turn-back cuffs

large brooch

pearls

large, turn-back fur cuffs

false undersleeves, padded and slashed

pomander case

small purse

quilted and embroidered underskirt

embroidered braid edging

fur trim

skirts worn over a farthingale (hoop or padded roll)

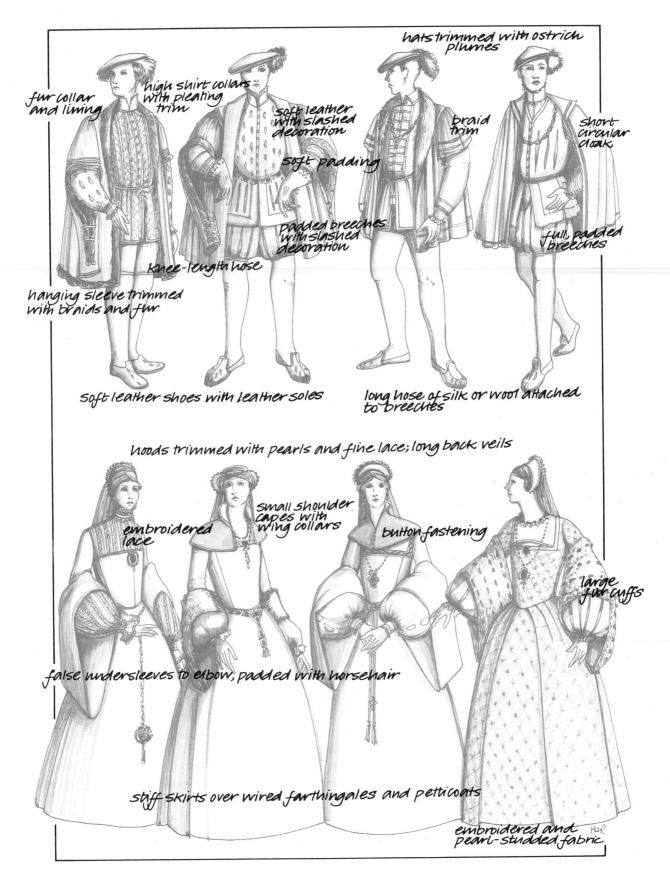

hats trimmed with ostrich plumes

fur collar and lining

high shirt collars with pleating trim

soft leather with slashed decoration

braid trim

short circular cloak

soft padding

padded breeches with slashed decoration

full, padded breeches

knee-length hose

hanging sleeve trimmed with braids and fur

soft leather shoes with leather soles

long hose of silk or wool attached to breeches

hoods trimmed with pearls and fine lace; long back veils

embroidered lace

small shoulder capes with wing collars

button fastening

large fur cuffs

false undersleeves to elbow, padded with horsehair

stiff skirts over wired farthingales and petticoats

embroidered and pearl-studded fabric

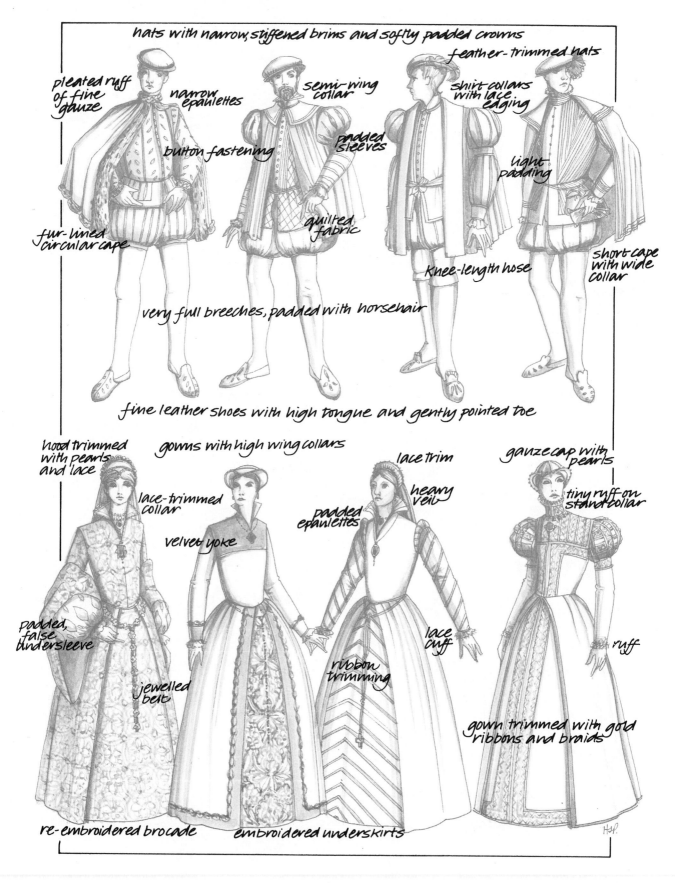

hats with narrow, stiffened brims and softly padded crowns

feather-trimmed hats

pleated ruff of fine gauze

narrow epaulettes

semi-wing collar

shirt collars with lace edging

button fastening

padded sleeves

light padding

fur-lined circular cape

quilted fabric

knee-length hose

short cape with wide collar

very full breeches, padded with horsehair

fine leather shoes with high tongue and gently pointed toe

hood trimmed with pearls and lace

gowns with high wing collars

lace trim

gauze cap with pearls

lace-trimmed collar

heavy veil

tiny ruff on stand collar

velvet yoke

padded epaulettes

padded, false undersleeve

lace cuff

ruff

jewelled belt

ribbon trimming

re-embroidered brocade

embroidered underskirts

gown trimmed with gold ribbons and braids

H.P.

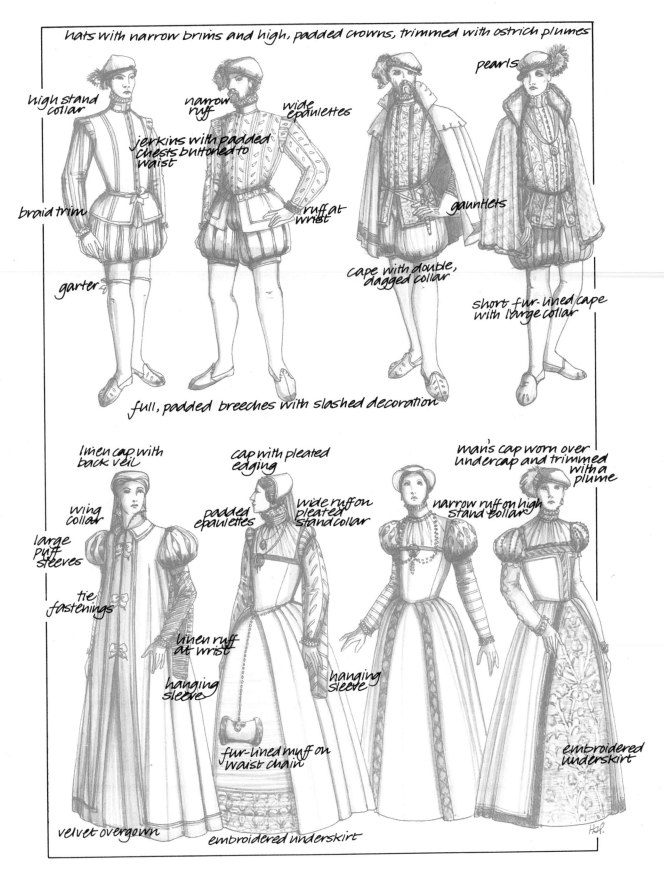

hats with narrow brims and high, padded crowns, trimmed with ostrich plumes

high stand collar

narrow ruff

wide epaulettes

pearls

jerkins with padded chests buttoned to waist

braid trim

ruff at wrist

gauntlets

garter

cape with double, dagged collar

short fur-lined cape with large collar

full, padded breeches with slashed decoration

linen cap with back veil

cap with pleated edging

man's cap worn over undercap and trimmed with a plume

wing collar

padded epaulettes

wide ruff on pleated stand collar

narrow ruff on high stand collar

large puff sleeves

tie fastenings

linen ruff at wrist

hanging sleeve

hanging sleeve

fur-lined muff on waist chain

embroidered underskirt

velvet overgown

embroidered underskirt

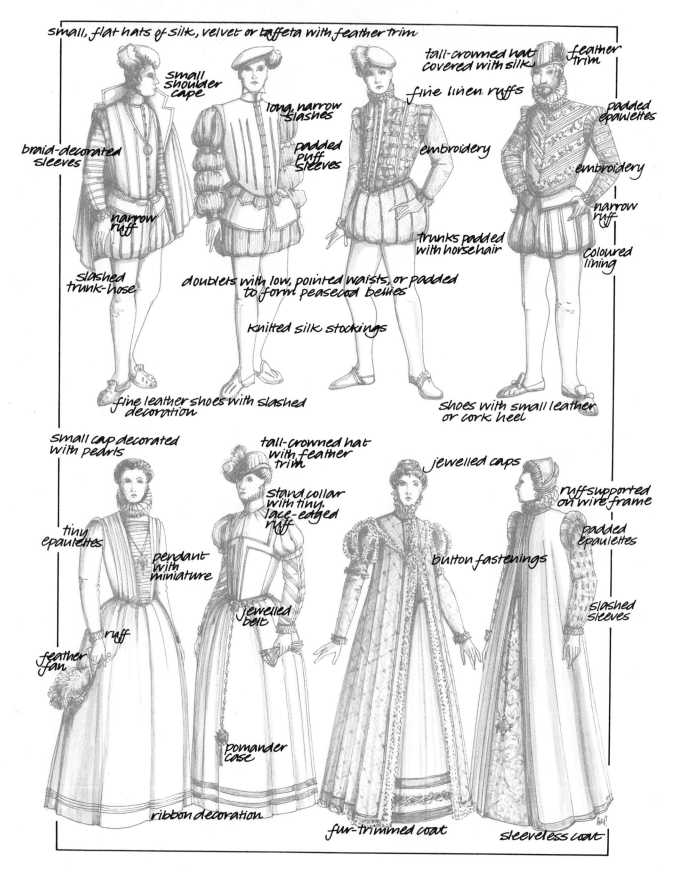

small, flat hats of silk, velvet or taffeta with feather trim

small shoulder cape

long, narrow slashes

tall-crowned hat covered with silk

feather trim

fine linen ruffs

padded epaulettes

braid-decorated sleeves

padded puff sleeves

embroidery

embroidery

narrow ruff

trunks padded with horsehair

narrow ruff

slashed trunk-hose

coloured lining

doublets with low, pointed waists, or padded to form peasecod bellies

knitted silk stockings

fine leather shoes with slashed decoration

shoes with small leather or cork heel

small cap decorated with pearls

tall-crowned hat with feather trim

jewelled caps

ruff supported on wire frame

tiny epaulettes

stand collar with tiny, lace-edged ruff

button fastenings

padded epaulettes

pendant with miniature

jewelled belt

slashed sleeves

ruff

feather fan

pomander case

ribbon decoration

fur-trimmed coat

sleeveless coat

tall-crowned hats, covered with fine fabric

tall hat with brooch trim and two feathers

ruff on fine wire frame

unpleated ruff on a fine wire frame

lace edging

braid-trimmed doublet

double epaulettes

peascod bellies

large buttons

wrist ruff

short-sleeveless jerkin with fur lining and trim

long panes to the knee

short stockings supported by garters

leather shoes with long tongues, soles and heels of leather or cork

small caps, trimmed with lace, pearls or jewels

tall-crowned hat with feather trim

brooch hair ornament

pearl-drop earrings

lace edging on collar

tiny ruff on stand collar

lace edging

slashed puff sleeves

tight bodices with low pointed waists

narrow ruff

jewelled belt

skirts worn over French farthingales (metal frames)

velvet coat lined and trimmed with fur

gowns with fine fur trim

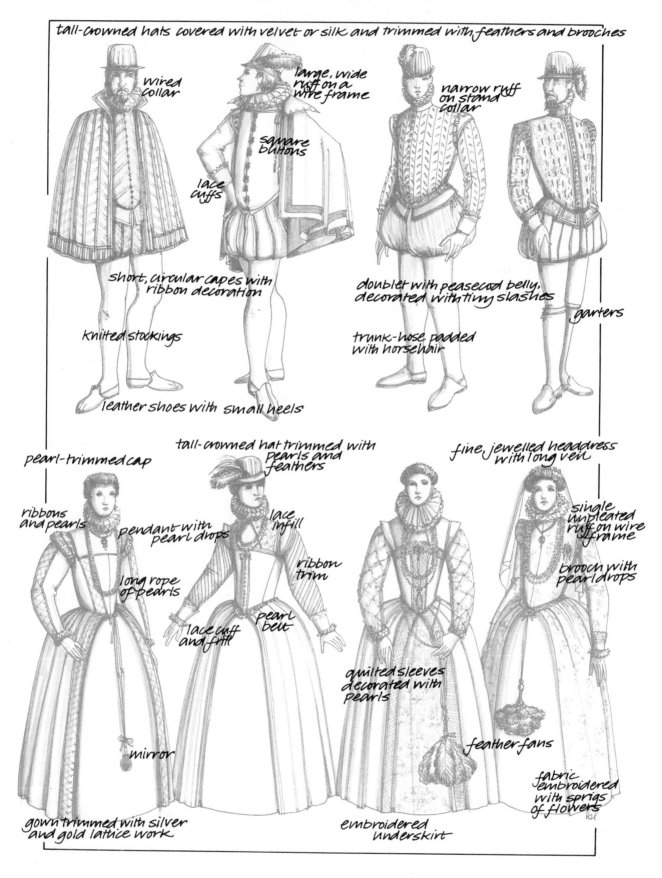

tall-crowned hats covered with velvet or silk and trimmed with feathers and brooches

wired collar

large, wide ruff on a wire frame

square buttons

lace cuffs

narrow ruff on stand collar

short, circular capes with ribbon decoration

doublet with peasecod belly, decorated with tiny slashes

garters

knitted stockings

trunk-hose padded with horsehair

leather shoes with small heels

pearl-trimmed cap

tall-crowned hat trimmed with pearls and feathers

fine, jewelled headdress with long veil

ribbons and pearls

pendant with pearl drops

lace infill

single unpleated ruff on wire frame

long rope of pearls

ribbon trim

brooch with pearl drops

lace cuff and frill

pearl belt

quilted sleeves decorated with pearls

mirror

feather fans

gown trimmed with silver and gold lattice work

embroidered underskirt

fabric embroidered with sprigs of flowers

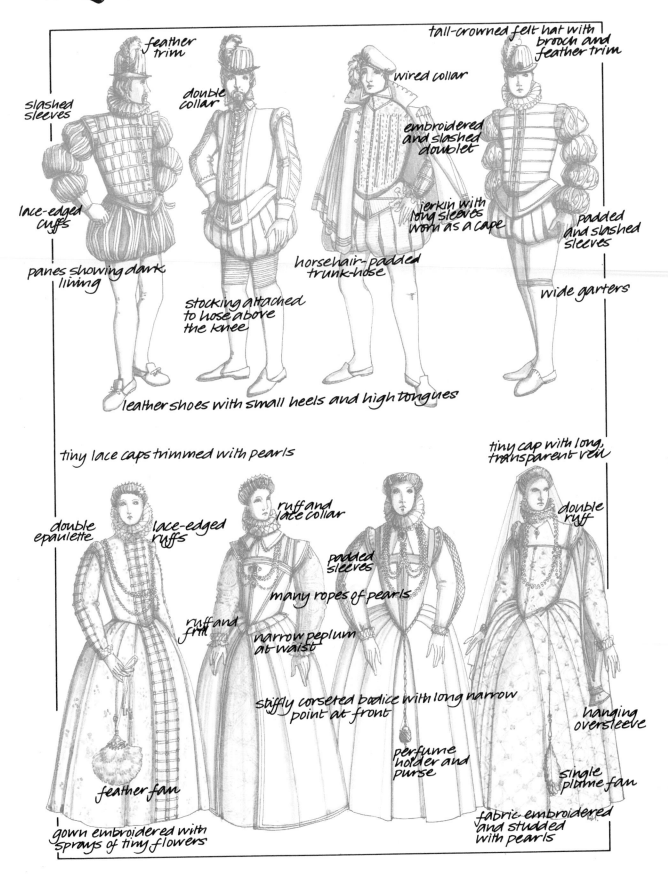

feather trim

tall-crowned felt hat with brooch and feather trim

slashed sleeves

double collar

wired collar

embroidered and slashed doublet

lace-edged cuffs

jerkin with long sleeves worn as a cape

padded and slashed sleeves

panes showing dark lining

horsehair-padded trunk-hose

wide garters

stocking attached to hose above the knee

leather shoes with small heels and high tongues

tiny lace caps trimmed with pearls

tiny cap with long, transparent veil

double epaulette

lace-edged ruffs

ruff and lace collar

double ruff

padded sleeves

many ropes of pearls

ruff and frill

narrow peplum at waist

stiffly corseted bodice with long narrow point at front

hanging oversleeve

perfume holder and purse

single plume fan

feather fan

fabric embroidered and studded with pearls

gown embroidered with sprays of tiny flowers

tall-crowned hats with feather trim

gold button trim

collar and ruff

wide epaulettes

wide, shallow-pleated ruff on a wire frame

flat, lace-edged collar

fine tucks

miniature on silk ribbon

large painted buttons

short circular cape

trunk-hose padded with horsehair or cotton wool

hose and stockings joined above knee

knitted silk stockings to the knee fastened with garters

long leather boots attached to trunk-hose with straps

small silk caps trimmed with gold ribbons and pearls

hair ornaments

miniature on velvet ribbon

pearl trim

flat, lace-edged ruff

wing collar from neck edge

ribbon-decorated bodice and sleeves

long pointed waist seams

narrow peplum

hanging sleeve

wide pleated peplum

pomander on fine chain

tiny bow

brooch

ribbon trim on hem

fine leather shoes with small, low heels

skirts worn a few inches off the ground

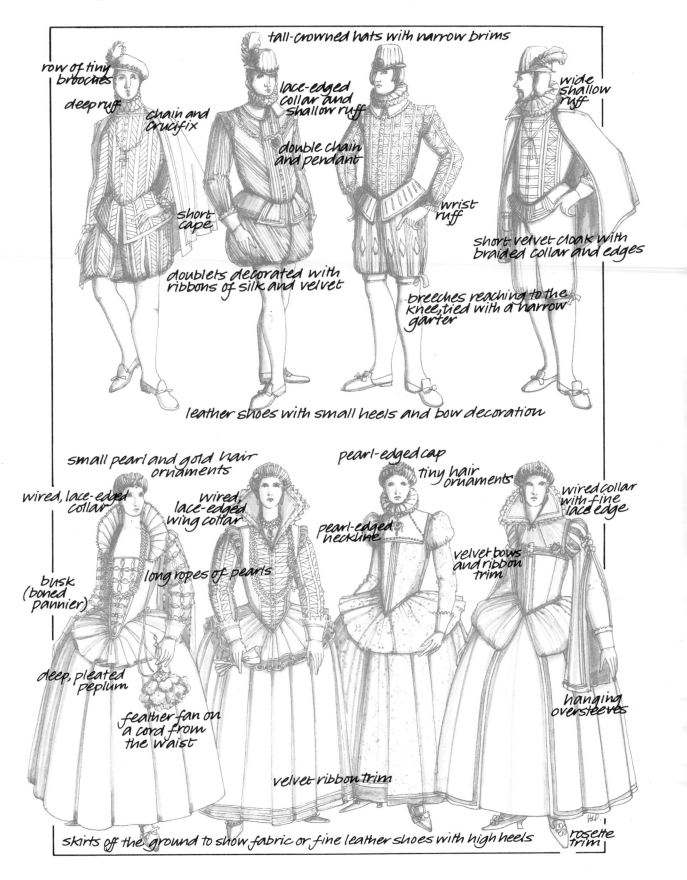

tall-crowned hats with narrow brims

row of tiny brooches

deep ruff

chain and crucifix

lace-edged collar and shallow ruff

double chain and pendant

wide shallow ruff

short cape

wrist ruff

short velvet cloak with braided collar and edges

doublets decorated with ribbons of silk and velvet

breeches reaching to the knee, tied with a narrow garter

leather shoes with small heels and bow decoration

small pearl and gold hair ornaments

pearl-edged cap

tiny hair ornaments

wired, lace-edged collar

wired, lace-edged wing collar

pearl-edged neckline

wired collar with fine lace edge

velvet bows and ribbon trim

busk (boned pannier)

long ropes of pearls

deep, pleated peplum

feather fan on a cord from the waist

hanging oversleeves

velvet ribbon trim

skirts off the ground to show fabric or fine leather shoes with high heels

rosette trim

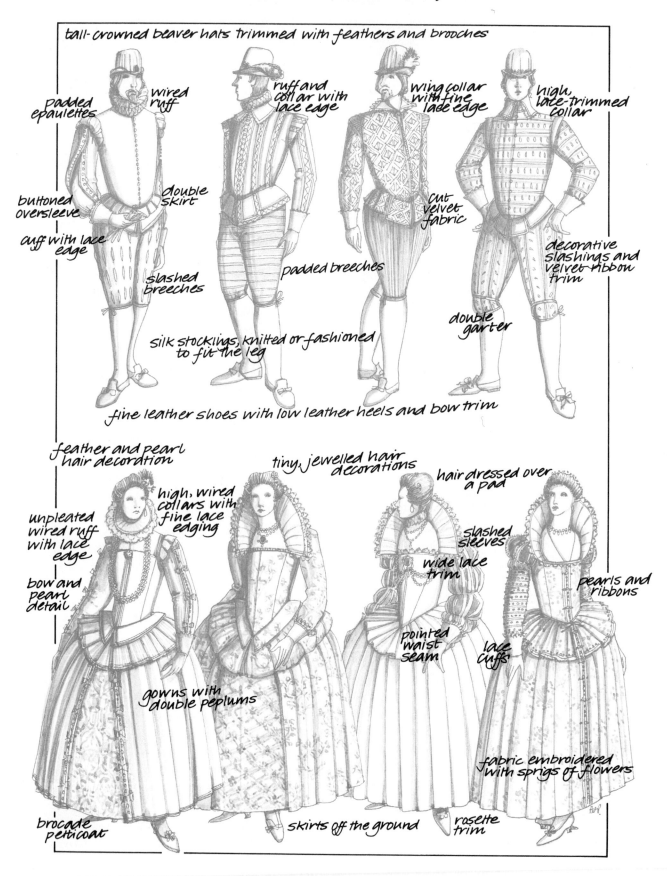

tall-crowned beaver hats trimmed with feathers and brooches

padded epaulettes

wired ruff

ruff and collar with lace edge

wing collar with fine lace edge

high, lace-trimmed collar

buttoned oversleeve

double skirt

cut velvet fabric

cuff with lace edge

decorative slashings and velvet ribbon trim

slashed breeches

padded breeches

double garter

silk stockings, knitted or fashioned to fit the leg

fine leather shoes with low leather heels and bow trim

feather and pearl hair decoration

tiny, jewelled hair decorations

hair dressed over a pad

unpleated wired ruff with lace edge

high, wired collars with fine lace edging

slashed sleeves

wide lace trim

pearls and ribbons

bow and pearl detail

pointed waist seam

lace cuffs

gowns with double peplums

brocade petticoat

skirts off the ground

rosette trim

fabric embroidered with sprigs of flowers

JAMES I · 1603~25

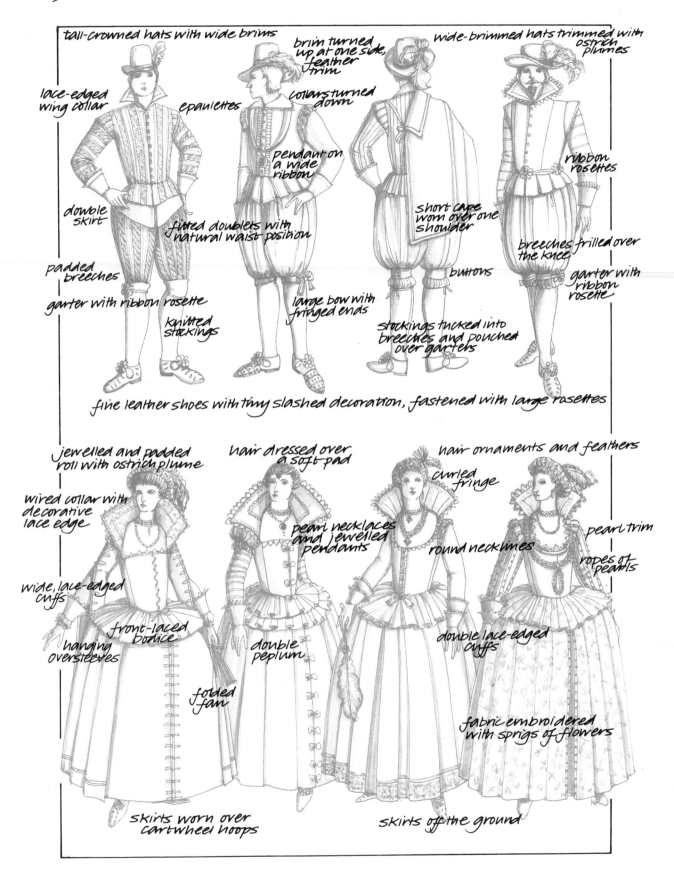

tall-crowned hats with wide brims

brim turned up at one side, feather trim

wide-brimmed hats trimmed with ostrich plumes

lace-edged wing collar

epaulettes

collars turned down

pendant on a wide ribbon

ribbon rosettes

double skirt

fitted doublets with natural waist position

short cape worn over one shoulder

breeches frilled over the knee

padded breeches

buttons

garter with ribbon rosette

garter with ribbon rosette

large bow with fringed ends

knitted stockings

stockings tucked into breeches and pouched over garters

fine leather shoes with tiny slashed decoration, fastened with large rosettes

jewelled and padded roll with ostrich plume

hair dressed over a soft pad

hair ornaments and feathers

wired collar with decorative lace edge

curled fringe

pearl necklaces and jewelled pendants

pearl trim

round necklines

ropes of pearls

wide, lace-edged cuffs

front-laced bodice

double peplum

double lace-edged cuffs

hanging oversleeves

folded fan

fabric embroidered with sprigs of flowers

skirts worn over cartwheel hoops

skirts off the ground

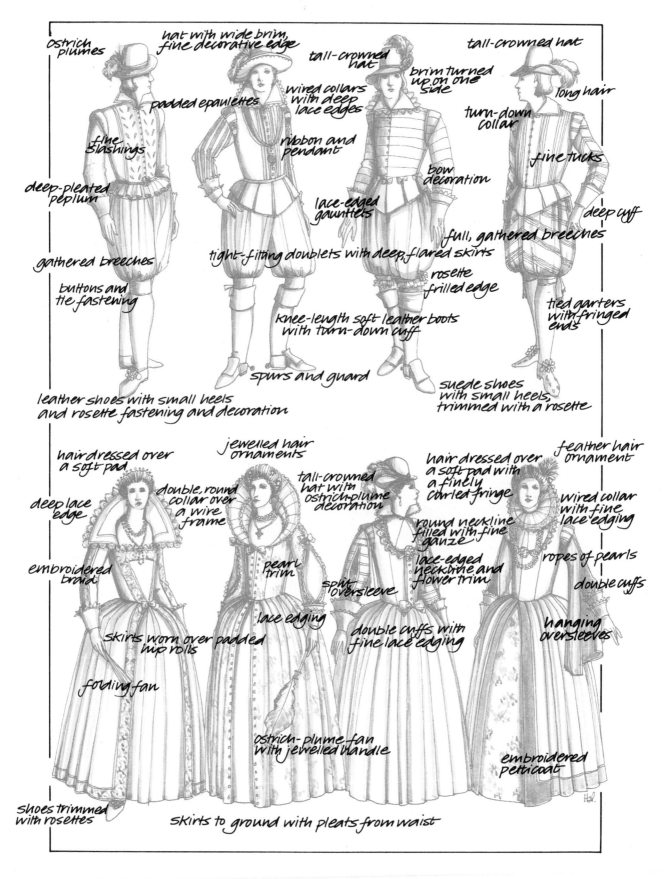

ostrich plumes

hat with wide brim, fine decorative edge

tall-crowned hat

tall-crowned hat

padded epaulettes

wired collars with deep lace edges

brim turned up on one side

long hair

turn-down collar

fine slashings

ribbon and pendant

fine tucks

deep-pleated peplum

bow decoration

deep cuff

lace-edged gauntlets

full, gathered breeches

gathered breeches

tight-fitting doublets with deep, flared skirts

rosette frilled edge

buttons and tie fastening

tied garters with fringed ends

knee-length soft leather boots with turn-down cuff

spurs and guard

suede shoes with small heels, trimmed with a rosette

leather shoes with small heels and rosette fastening and decoration

hair dressed over a soft pad

jewelled hair ornaments

feather hair ornament

double, round collar over a wire frame

tall-crowned hat with ostrich-plume decoration

hair dressed over a soft pad with a finely curled fringe

deep lace edge

wired collar with fine lace edging

embroidered braid

pearl trim

round neckline filled with fine gauze

ropes of pearls

split oversleeve

lace-edged neckline and flower trim

double cuffs

lace edging

skirts worn over padded hip rolls

hanging oversleeves

double cuffs with fine lace edging

folding fan

ostrich-plume fan with jewelled handle

embroidered petticoat

shoes trimmed with rosettes

skirts to ground with pleats from waist

CHARLES I · 1625~49

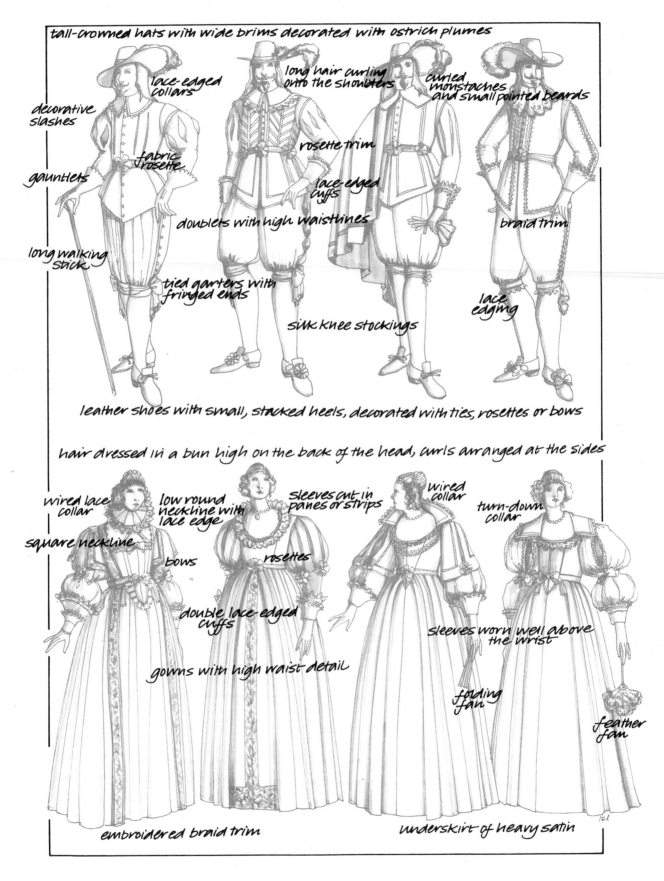

tall-crowned hats with wide brims decorated with ostrich plumes

lace-edged collars

long hair curling onto the shoulders

curled moustaches and small pointed beards

decorative slashes

rosette trim

fabric rosette

gauntlets

lace-edged cuffs

braid trim

doublets with high waistlines

long walking stick

tied garters with fringed ends

lace edging

silk knee stockings

leather shoes with small, stacked heels, decorated with ties, rosettes or bows

hair dressed in a bun high on the back of the head, curls arranged at the sides

wired lace collar

low round neckline with lace edge

sleeves cut in panes or strips

wired collar

turn-down collar

square neckline

bows

rosettes

double lace-edged cuffs

sleeves worn well above the wrist

gowns with high waist detail

folding fan

feather fan

embroidered braid trim

underskirt of heavy satin

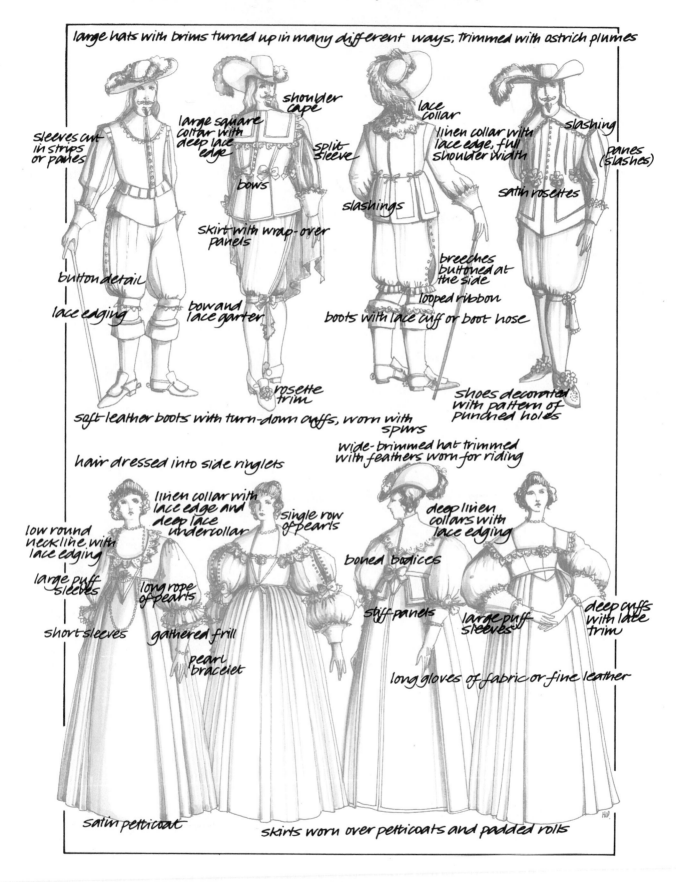

large hats with brims turned up in many different ways, trimmed with ostrich plumes

sleeves cut in strips or panes

large square collar with deep lace edge

shoulder cape

split sleeve

bows

lace collar

linen collar with lace edge, full shoulder width

slashing

panes (slashes)

satin rosettes

slashings

Skirt with wrap-over panels

breeches buttoned at the side

looped ribbon

button detail

lace edging

bow and lace garter

boots with lace cuff or boot hose

rosette trim

shoes decorated with pattern of punched holes

soft leather boots with turn-down cuffs, worn with spurs

wide-brimmed hat trimmed with feathers worn for riding

hair dressed into side ringlets

linen collar with lace edge and deep lace undercollar

single row of pearls

deep linen collars with lace edging

low round neckline with lace edging

large puff sleeves

boned bodices

long rope of pearls

short sleeves

gathered frill

stiff panels

large puff sleeves

deep cuffs with lace trim

pearl bracelet

long gloves of fabric or fine leather

satin petticoat

skirts worn over petticoats and padded rolls

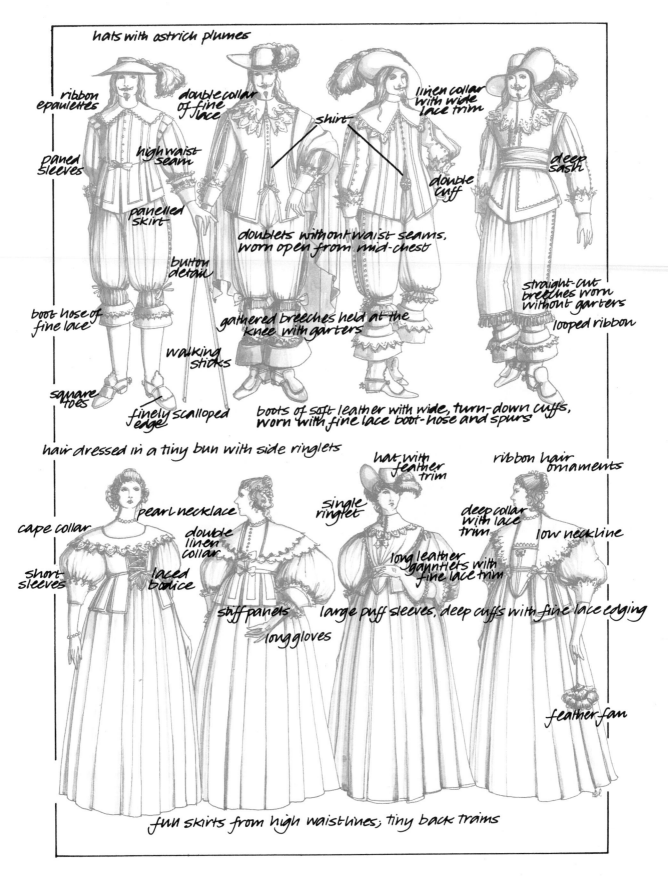

hats with ostrich plumes

ribbon epaulettes

double collar of fine lace

shirt

linen collar with wide lace trim

paned sleeves

high waist seam

deep sash

panelled skirt

double cuff

button detail

doublets without waist seams, worn open from mid-chest

boot hose of fine lace

straight-cut breeches worn without garters

gathered breeches held at the knee with garters

looped ribbon

walking sticks

square toes

finely scalloped edge

boots of soft leather with wide, turn-down cuffs, worn with fine lace boot-hose and spurs

hair dressed in a tiny bun with side ringlets

hat with feather trim

ribbon hair ornaments

single ringlet

deep collar with lace trim

cape collar

pearl necklace

low neckline

double linen collar

short sleeves

laced bodice

long leather gauntlets with fine lace trim

stiff panels

large puff sleeves, deep cuffs with fine lace edging

long gloves

feather fan

full skirts from high waistlines; tiny back trains

55

hat with wide brim

tall-crowned hats with narrow brims trimmed with ostrich plumes

linen collars, lace trim

long hair

lace and braid trim

lace collar

button and braid trim

shirt

ribbon trim

embroidered braid

short jacket

shirt with lace cuffs

doublets cut without a waist seam, buttoned to mid-chest

full gathered waist

straight-cut breeches worn without garters

ribbon decoration

button detail

lace

walking cane

looped ribbon

ribbon decoration

lace boot-hose

boots with deep, turn-down cuffs worn with boot-hose

hair in small bun, tiny side ringlets and curled fringe

low round neckline with lace edge

long side curls

double linen collar

wide cape collar

deep linen collar

lace collar

low, round neckline

tight sleeves to below elbow

long, boned bodice

gowns with boned bodices, skirts from natural waist position, overskirt looped to the back

small back train

gowns of silk satin, lace and velvet

COMMONWEALTH · 1649~60

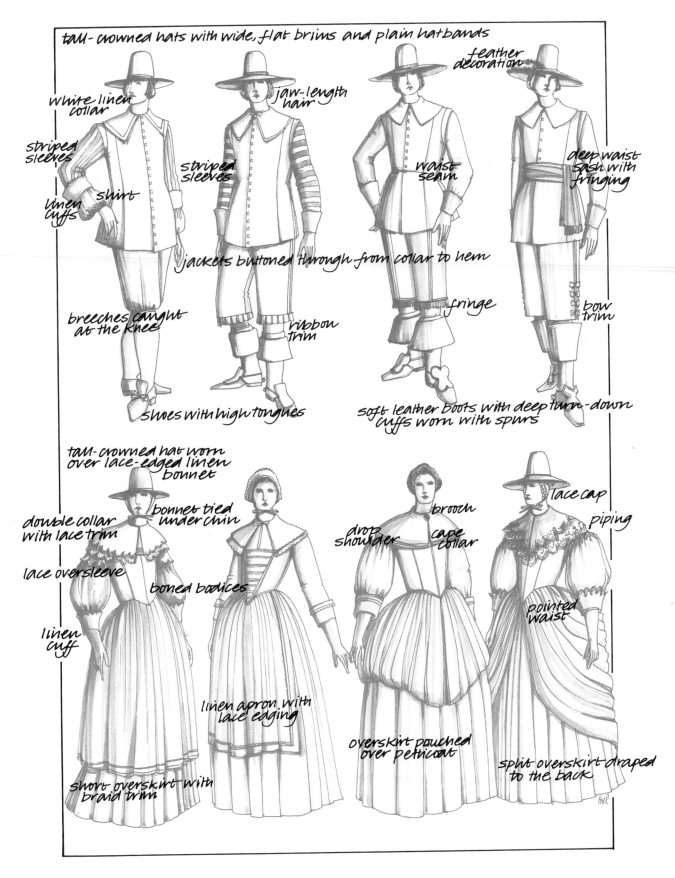

tall-crowned hats with wide, flat brims and plain hatbands

feather decoration

white linen collar

jaw-length hair

striped sleeves

striped sleeves

waist seam

deep waist sash with fringing

shirt

linen cuffs

jackets buttoned through from collar to hem

breeches caught at the knee

ribbon trim

fringe

bow trim

shoes with high tongues

soft leather boots with deep turn-down cuffs worn with spurs

tall-crowned hat worn over lace-edged linen bonnet

bonnet tied under chin

brooch

lace cap

double collar with lace trim

drop shoulder

cape collar

piping

lace oversleeve

boned bodices

linen cuff

pointed waist

linen apron with lace edging

overskirt pouched over petticoat

split overskirt draped to the back

short overskirt with braid trim

CHARLES II · 1660~85

tall-crowned hats with wide brims decorated with feathers and ribbons

Long hair to the shoulders

ribbon trim

French periwig

lace-bordered cravats

short sleeves

full shirt sleeves with lace frills

ribbon trim

pocket

petticoat breeches worn over full, gathered underbreeches

knee-length cloak

ribbons

boot-hose

long leather boots with deep cuffs

fabric bows

square-toed shoes with high heels and high tongues

tall-crowned hat trimmed with feathers

ringlets padded with false hair

hair dressed into deep side ringlets

ribbons

lace trim

pearl necklace

low, scooped necklines

puff sleeves

boned bodice

full sleeves with fine lace cuffs

heavily boned bodices

deep lace cuffs

overskirts looped up to each side

overskirt looped up to one side

petticoat or underskirt

58

Wide-brimmed hat with shallow crown

brim turned up at the front

hats trimmed with large ostrich plumes

French periwigs

lace neckcloth

short jacket with deep cuffs

ribbon epaulettes

shirt

braid trim

petticoat breeches trimmed with looped ribbon

full breeches with ribbon trim

long walking cane

boot-hose worn with silk stockings

silk stockings fastened under breeches

walking cane

shoes with high tongues and decorated with stiff bows

hair with centre parting curled on each side with added false ringlets

fine gauze veil

puff sleeves decorated with large bows

low, scooped necklines

deep lace collar

veil tucked into neckline

lace frills

tight sleeves with deep cuff and frill to wrist

puff sleeves with bow trim

lace frill

overskirt looped back to waist

embroidered braids

overskirt split and gathered to the back

petticoats

decorated petticoats

hats with feather and ribbon trim

wide hats with large feathers

long, curled hair wigs

bows and ribbons

brooch

fine lace cravats

deep cuffs

fine pleating

circular travelling cape

buttoned pockets

long coats with front button fastening

ribbon-decorated petticoat breeches

rosette

breeches gathered into a cuff or band

ribbon detail

lace boot-hose

walking cane

silk stockings worn under full gathered breeches

shoes with large bows

stiff, narrow bows

walking cane

hair dressed from a centre parting into wide side ringlets and a single shoulder ringlet

ribbon decoration

lace collar

ribbon epaulettes

deep lace collar

gauze infill

large brooch

bow trim

deeply scooped necklines

lace cuff

folding fan

overskirt looped back to form small back train

looped-up overskirt

full underskirts or petticoats

gowns with full skirts made from silks and satins

HP.

CHARLES II · 1660~85 *(continued)*

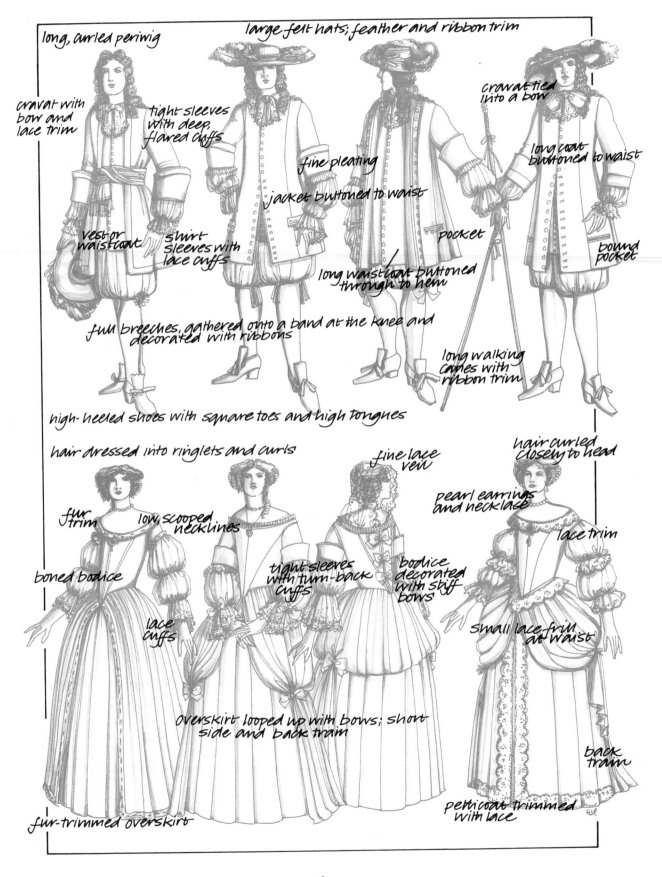

long, curled periwig

large felt hats; feather and ribbon trim

cravat tied into a bow

cravat with bow and lace trim

tight sleeves with deep, flared cuffs

fine pleating

long coat buttoned to waist

jacket buttoned to waist

vest or waistcoat

shirt sleeves with lace cuffs

pocket

bound pocket

long waistcoat buttoned through to hem

full breeches, gathered onto a band at the knee and decorated with ribbons

long walking canes with ribbon trim

high-heeled shoes with square toes and high tongues

hair dressed into ringlets and curls

fine lace veil

hair curled closely to head

pearl earrings and necklace

fur trim

low, scooped necklines

lace trim

boned bodice

tight sleeves with turn-back cuffs

bodice decorated with stiff bows

lace cuffs

small lace frill at waist

overskirt looped up with bows; short side and back train

back train

fur-trimmed overskirt

petticoat trimmed with lace

wide-brimmed hats trimmed with ribbons and feathers

wigs with centre parting of arranged into stiff, formal curls

bow tie and lace cravat

embroidered braid

long waistcoat buttoned through to hem

coat buttoned to the waist

long vest or waistcoat

deep cuffs, braid trim

lace-edged shirt-cuffs

breeches gathered at the knee

coats split at centre back and side seams, with decorative buttons and buttonholes

long walking sticks

leather shoes with tall tongues, high red heels and buckle trims

hair with centre-front parting, arranged into tight curls and ringlets

cap with loops of ribbon

long ties

draped necklines

tight sleeves with turn-back cuffs

heavily boned bodices

lace-edged undersleeves

folding fan

overskirts looped up and back to show braided petticoats

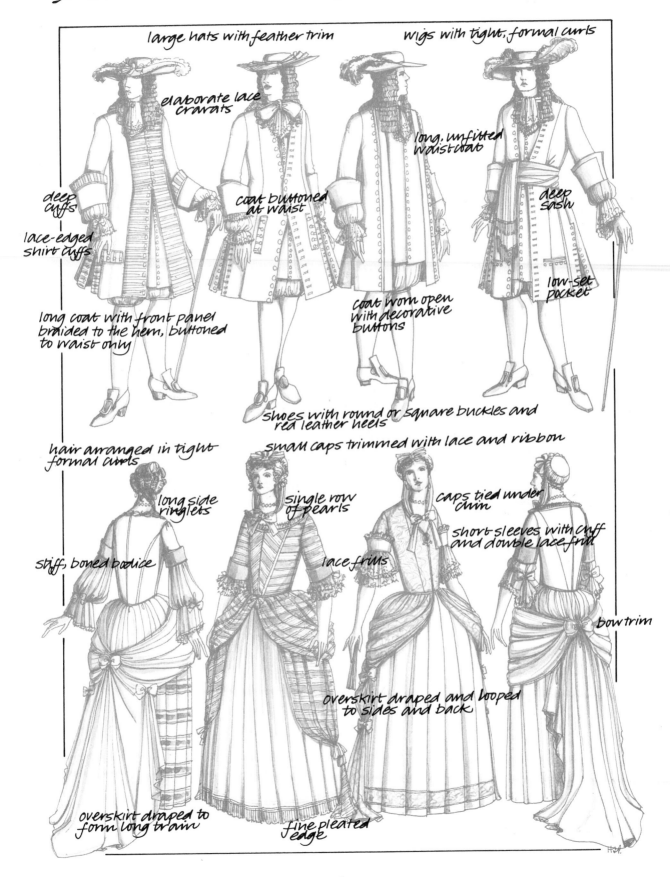

large hats with feather trim

wigs with tight, formal curls

elaborate lace cravats

deep cuffs

lace-edged shirt cuffs

coat buttoned at waist

long, unfitted waistcoat

deep sash

low-set pocket

long coat with front panel braided to the hem, buttoned to waist only

coat worn open with decorative buttons

shoes with round or square buckles and red leather heels

hair arranged in tight formal curls

long side ringlets

small caps trimmed with lace and ribbon

single row of pearls

caps tied under chin

short sleeves with cuff and double lace frill

stiff, boned bodice

lace frills

bow trim

overskirt draped and looped to sides and back

overskirt draped to form long train

fine pleated edge

WILLIAM AND MARY · 1689–1702

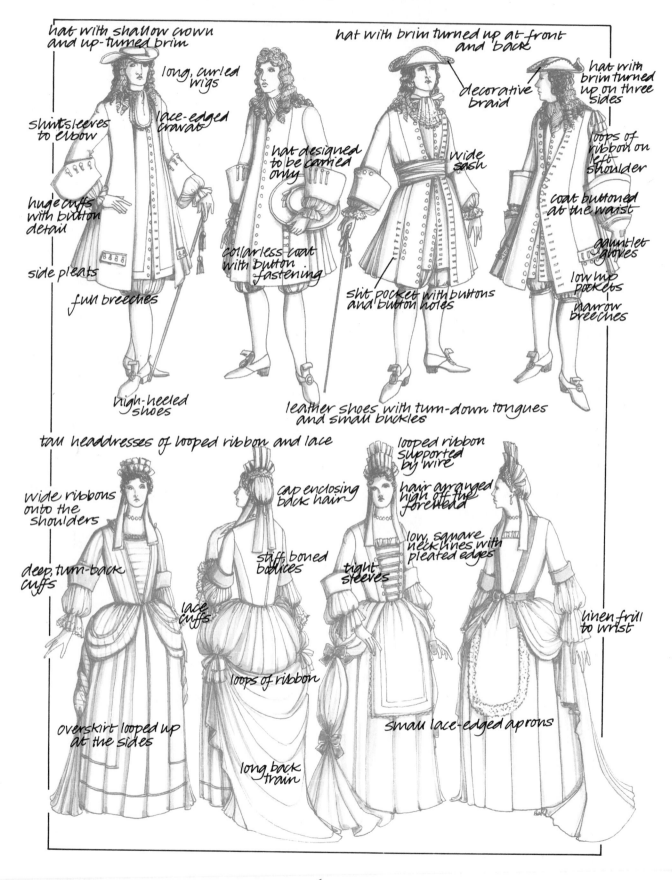

hat with shallow crown and up-turned brim

long, curled wigs

hat with brim turned up at front and back

decorative braid

hat with brim turned up on three sides

shirt sleeves to elbow

lace-edged cravats

hat designed to be carried only

wide sash

loops of ribbon on left shoulder

huge cuffs with button detail

coat buttoned at the waist

side pleats

collarless coat with button fastening

gauntlet gloves

full breeches

slit pocket with buttons and button holes

low hip pockets

narrow breeches

high-heeled shoes

leather shoes with turn-down tongues and small buckles

tall headdresses of looped ribbon and lace

looped ribbon supported by wire

wide ribbons onto the shoulders

cap enclosing back hair

hair arranged high off the forehead

deep, turn-back cuffs

stiff boned bodices

tight sleeves

low, square necklines with pleated edges

lace cuffs

linen frill to wrist

loops of ribbon

overskirt looped up at the sides

small lace-edged aprons

long back train

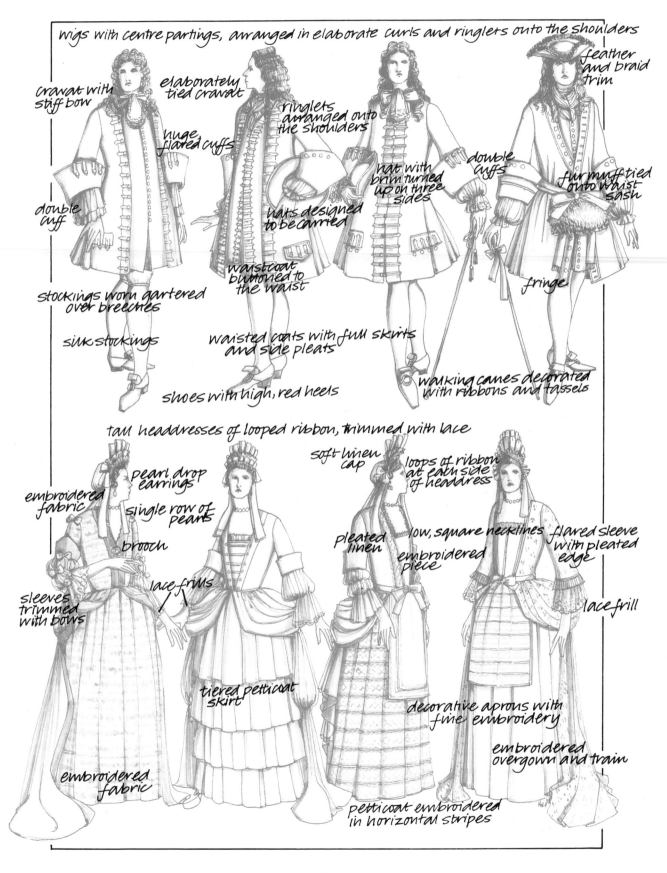

wigs with centre partings, arranged in elaborate curls and ringlets onto the shoulders

cravat with stiff bow

elaborately tied cravat

ringlets arranged onto the shoulders

feather and braid trim

huge flared cuffs

hat with brim turned up on three sides

double cuffs

double cuff

hats designed to be carried

fur muff tied onto waist sash

waistcoat buttoned to the waist

stockings worn gartered over breeches

silk stockings

waisted coats with full skirts and side pleats

fringe

shoes with high, red heels

walking canes decorated with ribbons and tassels

tall headdresses of looped ribbon, trimmed with lace

pearl drop earrings

soft linen cap

loops of ribbon at each side of headdress

embroidered fabric

single row of pearls

pleated linen

low, square necklines

flared sleeve with pleated edge

embroidered piece

brooch

lace frills

sleeves trimmed with bows

lace frill

tiered petticoat skirt

decorative aprons with fine embroidery

embroidered overgown and train

embroidered fabric

petticoat embroidered in horizontal stripes

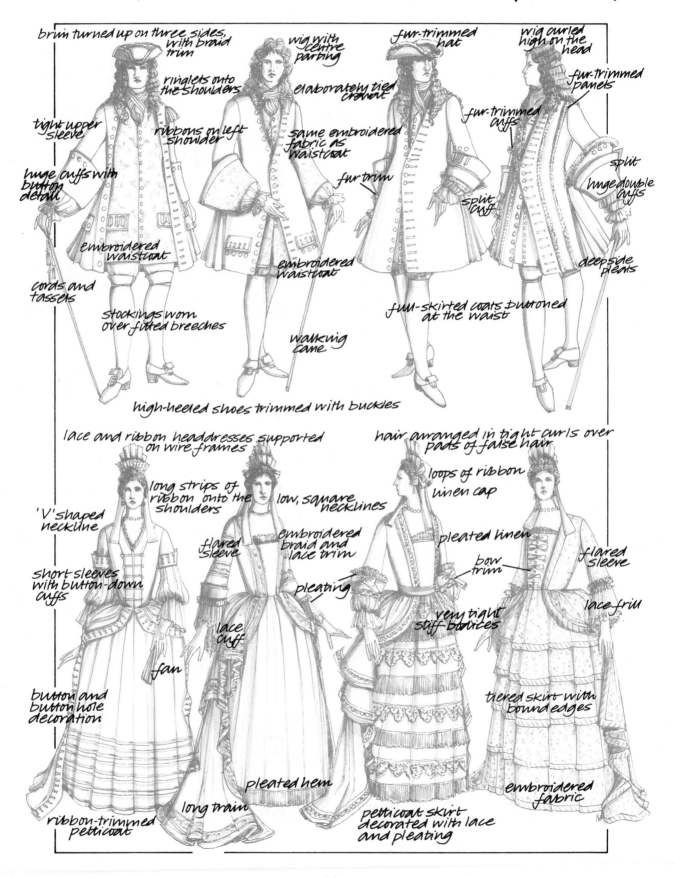

brim turned up on three sides, with braid trim

ringlets onto the shoulders

tight upper sleeve

ribbons on left shoulder

huge cuffs with button detail

embroidered waistcoat

cords and tassels

stockings worn over fitted breeches

wig with centre parting

elaborately tied cravat

same embroidered fabric as waistcoat

fur trim

embroidered waistcoat

walking cane

fur-trimmed hat

fur-trimmed cuffs

split cuff

full-skirted coats buttoned at the waist

wig curled high on the head

fur-trimmed panels

split huge double cuffs

deep side pleats

high-heeled shoes trimmed with buckles

lace and ribbon headdresses supported on wire frames

'V' shaped neckline

long strips of ribbon onto the shoulders

short sleeves with button-down cuffs

flared sleeve

low, square necklines

embroidered braid and lace trim

lace cuff

fan

pleating

button and button hole decoration

ribbon-trimmed petticoat

long train

pleated hem

hair arranged in tight curls over pads of false hair

loops of ribbon

linen cap

pleated linen

bow trim

very tight stiff bodices

petticoat skirt decorated with lace and pleating

flared sleeve

lace frill

tiered skirt with bound edges

embroidered fabric

ANNE · 1702-14

wigs arranged high on the head in large curls

ringlets

braid trim

lace handkerchief

came suspended from ribbons

large buttons

brim turned up at front and back

large cravats, some with tassel ends

waist seam

fur muff

fitted breeches to the knee, often velvet

waistcoat fastened at the waist only

formal curls

straight hair at back of wig

small tight curls

huge cuffs with decorative buttonholes

side pleats

back vent with braid and button trim

high heels

shoes with large buckles and square toes

small cap with loops of ribbon

hair with centre parting

ringlets onto the shoulders

folding fan

ringlets

embroidered braid

low, square necklines with pleated edges

lace frills

low, scooped neckline

stiffly boned bodice with ribbon and bow trim

fur muff

lace-edged apron

overskirts looped up and back with long trailing panels

embroidered fabric

full skirts worn over petticoats and pads

quilted and embroidered petticoat

67

GEORGE I · 1714~27

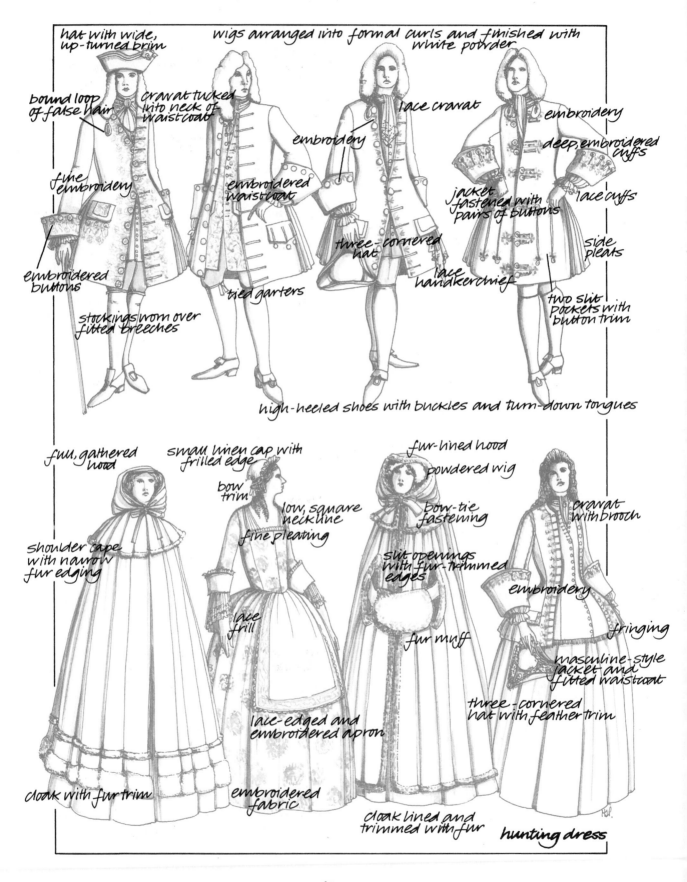

hat with wide, up-turned brim

wigs arranged into formal curls and finished with white powder

bound loop of false hair

cravat tucked into neck of waistcoat

lace cravat

embroidery

fine embroidery

embroidery

deep, embroidered cuffs

embroidered waistcoat

jacket fastened with pairs of buttons

lace cuffs

embroidered buttons

three-cornered hat

side pleats

lace handkerchief

tied garters

two slit pockets with button trim

stockings worn over fitted breeches

high-heeled shoes with buckles and turn-down tongues

full, gathered hood

small linen cap with frilled edge

fur-lined hood

powdered wig

bow trim

low, square neckline

cravat with brooch

shoulder cape with narrow fur edging

fine pleating

bow-tie fastening

slit openings with fur-trimmed edges

embroidery

lace frill

fur muff

fringing

masculine-style jacket and fitted waistcoat

three-cornered hat with feather trim

cloak with fur trim

lace-edged and embroidered apron

embroidered fabric

cloak lined and trimmed with fur

hunting dress

hat with brim turned up front and back

braided edge

full, powdered wigs

wigs with straight hair at the back

large loop of stiff hair

bow

powdered wig

decorative braid over construction seams

tail of wig

embroidered braid and button holes

cuffs embroidered to match waistcoat

button trim

decorative buttons

embroidered buttons

embroidered waistcoat

decorative buttons and buttonholes

quilted waistcoat

coats with back split

coat with rich embroidery

walking cane

shoes with high heels, square toes and turn-down tongues

small caps trimmed with lace, frills, pleats and bows

powdered wig

powdered wig

tight sleeves

low, square neckline

pleating

self frill and frill of lace

pleats from embroidered yoke

tight bodice

draped cuff with bow trim

tight underbodice

lace frills

overdress with a pleated sack back

loose overdress caught with bows at front

embroidered braid edging

embroidered fabrics

pleated sack-backed gown

small train

GEORGE II · 1727~60

wigs dressed away from the face, with side curls and ringlets down the back tied in a large bow

soft side curls

bow over cravat

lace

high-buttoned waistcoats

wigs powdered white

waistcoat buttons to waist only

ends of hair ribbon

two side curls

buttons in pairs

embroidered fabric

sleeves to wrist with turn-back cuffs

pockets set at hip level

button fastenings

short waistcoat

three-cornered hat

embroidery

walking cane

rounded tongues

large buckles

leather shoes with flat heels

small linen caps with lace edging

straw hat with wide brim

lace edging

low, square neckline

pleated from neckline

deep, inverted pleat

ribbon ties

taffeta bows

cuffs

deep pleat

short 'sack' caught up to one side

striped taffeta

open gown caught up and back

quilted and embroidered petticoat

embroidered fabric

sack-backed dress

small train

skirt off the ground

70

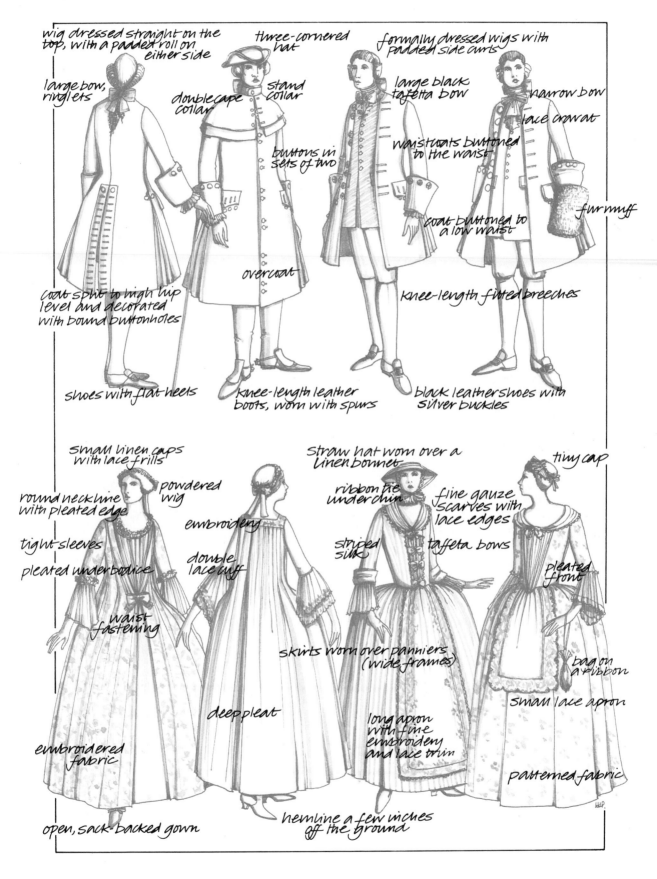

wig dressed straight on the top, with a padded roll on either side

three-cornered hat

formally dressed wigs with padded side curls

large bow, ringlets

double cape collar

stand collar

large black taffeta bow

narrow bow

lace cravat

buttons in sets of two

waistcoats buttoned to the waist

coat buttoned to a low waist

fur muff

coat split to high hip level and decorated with bound buttonholes

overcoat

knee-length fitted breeches

shoes with flat heels

knee-length leather boots, worn with spurs

black leather shoes with silver buckles

small linen caps with lace frills

powdered wig

Straw hat worn over a linen bonnet

tiny cap

round neckline with pleated edge

embroidery

ribbon tie under chin

fine gauze scarves with lace edges

tight sleeves

double lace cuff

striped silk

taffeta bows

pleated front

pleated underbodice

waist fastening

skirts worn over panniers (wide frames)

bag on a ribbon

deep pleat

long apron with fine embroidery and lace trim

small lace apron

embroidered fabric

patterned fabric

open, sack-backed gown

hemline a few inches off the ground

hats with up-turned, pleated brims

wig, powdered and dressed into formal side curls

three-cornered hat

large buttons

high buttons

tight sleeves

large bow

tight sleeves

quilted and embroidered waistcoat

embroidered waistcoat

cuff fitted to wrist

braided waistcoat

rounded ends

short waistcoat

buttons

braided coat

breeches with fitted band at the knee

button fastening on breeches

fine silk stockings

flat-heeled shoes with high, round tongues and large silver buckles

small linen cap, with lace trim

powdered wig

hair or wig dressed over pads

low neckline

pleated taffeta

artificial flowers

square neckline

ribbon

bow trim

lace and tucks

stiff bows

fine tucks

narrow cuff with bow trim

folding fan

striped fabric

wide panniers

lace trim

long apron with embroidery and lace

tiny apron with very fine embroidery

embroidered fabric

deep pleat

lace and tucks

quilted and embroidered petticoats

train

quilted petticoat with frilled hem

GEORGE III · 1760~1820 (i) c.1760~70

wigs dressed away from the face, with long side curls

shirt collar

shirt

stand collar

small collar

braided waistcoat

high-buttoned waistcoat

short double and single-breasted waistcoat

double-breasted waistcoat

narrow cuffs

short waistcoat

flap pockets, button trim

small cuff

leather gloves

fitted breeches

coat with braid trim

buckle

button fastening

fitted silk stockings

walking cane

leather boots

knee-length leather boots

soft leather shoes with flat heels, rounded tongues and silver buckles

tiny cap on padded wig

hair or wigs dressed over high pads or cages

linen cap with lace edging

neckband of ribbon and pleated silk

square neckline

fine linen scarf

folding fan

low, square neckline

lace edging

brooch

shoulder scarf

lace and pleated silk

short sack-backed gown

embroidered apron

quilted petticoat

open sack-backed gown

small train

skirts decorated with ruched and pleated silk

73

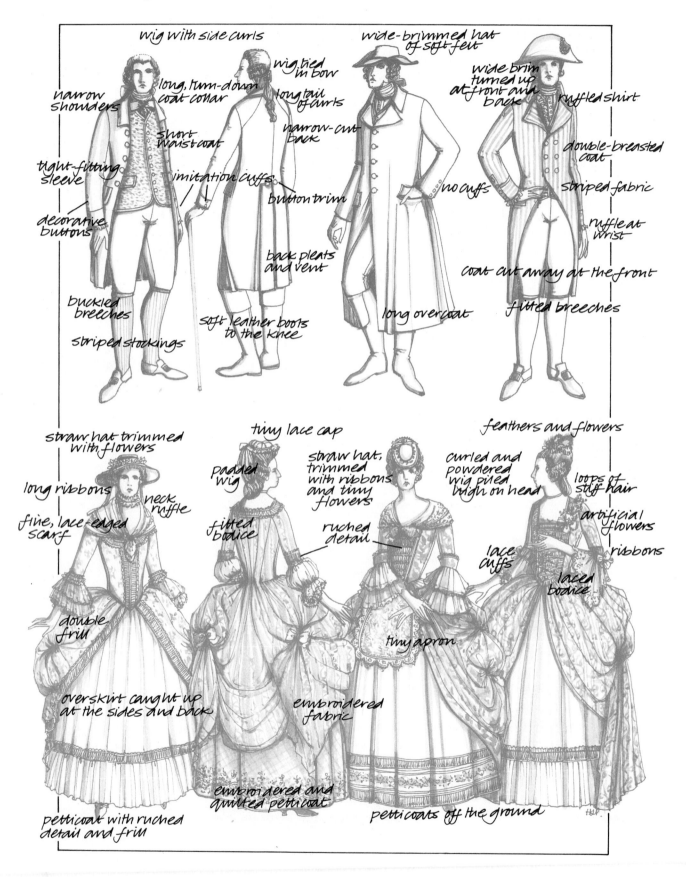

wig with side curls

long, turn-down coat collar

narrow shoulders

short waistcoat

tight-fitting sleeve

imitation cuffs

decorative buttons

buckled breeches

striped stockings

wig tied in bow

long tail of curls

narrow-cut back

button trim

back pleats and vent

soft leather boots to the knee

wide-brimmed hat of stiff felt

no cuffs

long overcoat

wide brim turned up at front and back

ruffled shirt

double-breasted coat

striped fabric

ruffle at wrist

coat cut away at the front

fitted breeches

straw hat trimmed with flowers

long ribbons

neck ruffle

fine, lace-edged scarf

double frill

overskirt caught up at the sides and back

petticoat with ruched detail and frill

tiny lace cap

padded wig

fitted bodice

embroidered and quilted petticoat

straw hat, trimmed with ribbons and tiny flowers

ruched detail

tiny apron

embroidered fabric

petticoats off the ground

feathers and flowers

curled and powdered wig piled high on head

lace cuffs

laced bodice

loops of stiff hair

artificial flowers

ribbons

felt hat with wide brim

high stand collars

waistcoat

double-breasted fastening

waistcoat

breeches with 'fall front' opening

coat cut away at the front

slim-fitting leather boots

boots of fine, soft leather with very flat heels

short, curled hair

striped coat

frill of shirt

false cuff and strap opening

button opening

tall-crowned hats with narrow brims

cravat tied in a large bow

three rows of buttons on waistcoat

three-tier cape collar

buttoned to waist

leather gloves

long overcoat with full skirt

flat-heeled leather pumps with bow decoration

brim turned up at each side

waistcoat with collar

double-breasted waistcoat

narrow, sloping shoulder line

jacket cut away above the natural waistline

tight sleeves

fitted breeches

ribbon garters

striped stockings with embroidered 'clocks'

powdered wig or hair, with long side ringlets

lace-edged scarf

tight sleeves

embroidered fabric

pleated decoration

large hood with lace edging

full-length cloak gathered from the neck

lacing

leather gloves

fur muff

fringed hem

hat with large brim and tiny crown

feathers

softly curled hair

lace scarf

flowers

ribbon at the throat

ribbon on natural waist position

tight sleeves

striped silk

stiff ribbon bows

long gloves

scarf tied at the back

frilled edge

large fur muff

fabric embroidered with sprigs of flowers

tall-crowned hat with curled brim

looped ribbon

three-tier cape collar

fitted into waist

button trim

overcoat

open vent to waist

tall hat with shallow brim

buckle trim

large bow

short, curled hair

tall stand collar

wide, pointed revers

tight sleeves

fur cuff

leather gloves

striped silk stockings

waistcoat collar

shirt-frill

button fastening

tall-crowned hat wide wide brim

high-buttoned waistcoat

double-breasted jacket

striped fabric

tight sleeves

buttons

slim-fitting breeches

leather pumps with bows or buckles

hat trimmed with ribbons

fine lace

brooch

ribbon belt

long lace frill

ribbon decoration

long walking cane

small hat with tall crown

hair decorated with ribbons

feathers and ribbons

draped shoulder scarf

flowers

tight sleeves

wide belt

gathered bodice

lace oversleeve

pearl necklace

high waist position

deep belt

draped turban

feather and brooch trim

large fur muff

fur-trimmed coat

slight back train

pleated hemlines

lace overskirt

hemlines just off the ground

hats with tall crowns

hat with curled brim

shirt collar

large bow-tied cravat

short hair

small tied bow

stand collar

high collar

narrow shoulders

contrast fabric collar and revers with matching sleeve cuffs

wide revers

gathered sleeve head

double-breasted waistcoat

tight sleeves

double-breasted jacket

button trim

imitation cuff

button opening

leather gloves

knee-length overcoat

walking cane

trousers with a braided seam

ankle-length trousers

long leather boots

low-cut leather pumps

straw bonnets trimmed with ribbons and flowers

small silk parasol

straw bonnet with ribbon trim

long curls

ribbon ties

gathered sleeve

puff sleeve

low neckline

square neckline

high waist sash

elbow-length sleeves

stole with pleated edge

tight undersleeve

kid gloves

long stole with gathered edge

hip-length jacket

small bag

open gown

embroidered decoration

parasol

striped fabric

embroidered fabric

fine, printed muslin

pleated hem

skirt hems off the ground

flat pumps

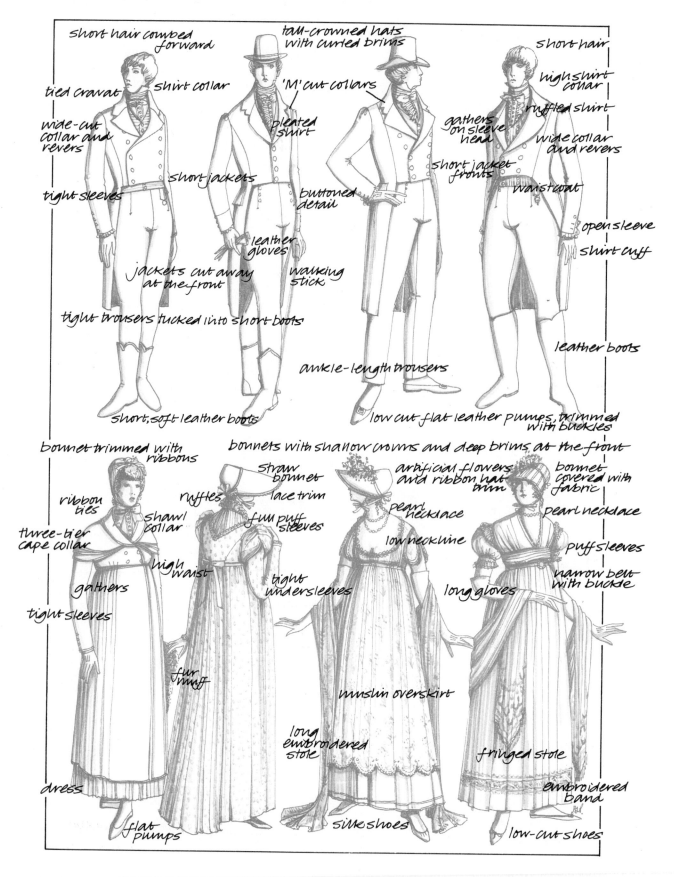

short hair combed forward

tall-crowned hats with curled brims

short hair

tied cravat

shirt collar

'M' cut collars

high shirt collar

wide-cut collar and revers

pleated shirt

gathers on sleeve head

ruffled shirt

tight sleeves

short jackets

buttoned detail

short jacket fronts

wide collar and revers

waistcoat

leather gloves

open sleeve

shirt cuff

jackets cut away at the front

walking stick

tight trousers tucked into short boots

leather boots

ankle-length trousers

short, soft leather boots

low cut flat leather pumps, trimmed with buckles

bonnet trimmed with ribbons

bonnets with shallow crowns and deep brims at the front

ribbon ties

straw bonnet

lace trim

artificial flowers and ribbon hat trim

bonnet covered with fabric

shawl collar

full puff sleeves

pearl necklace

pearl necklace

three-tier cape collar

high waist

low neckline

puff sleeves

gathers

tight undersleeves

long gloves

narrow belt with buckle

tight sleeves

fur trim

muslin overskirt

long embroidered stole

fringed stole

dress

flat pumps

silk shoes

low-cut shoes

embroidered band

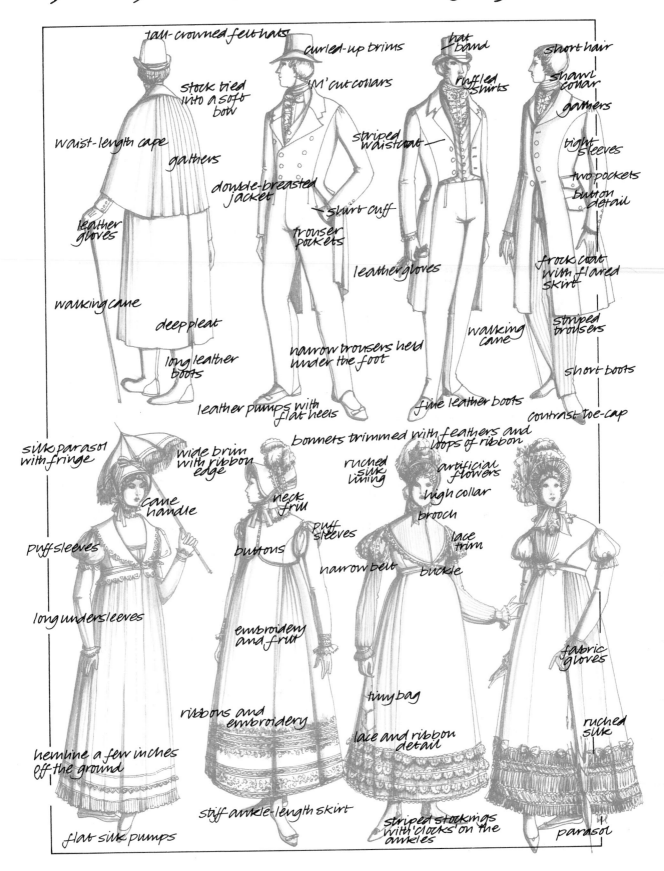

tall-crowned felt hats

curled-up brims

hat band

short hair

stock tied into a soft bow

'M' cut collars

ruffled shirts

shawl collar

waist-length cape

gathers

striped waistcoat

gathers

double-breasted jacket

tight sleeves

two pockets

button detail

skirt cuff

leather gloves

trouser pockets

leather gloves

frock coat with flared skirt

walking cane

deep pleat

walking cane

striped trousers

long leather boots

narrow trousers held under the foot

short boots

leather pumps with flat heels

fine leather boots

contrast toe-cap

silk parasol with fringe

wide brim with ribbon edge

bonnets trimmed with feathers and loops of ribbon

ruched silk lining

artificial flowers

cane handle

neck frill

high collar

puff sleeves

puff sleeves

brooch

long undersleeves

buttons

narrow belt

lace trim

buckle

embroidery and frill

tiny bag

fabric gloves

ribbons and embroidery

lace and ribbon detail

ruched silk

hemline a few inches off the ground

flat silk pumps

stiff ankle-length skirt

striped stockings with 'clocks' on the ankles

parasol

GEORGE IV · 1820~30

tall-crowned top hats with shallow, curled brims

curled hair

short hair

side whiskers

wing collar on shirt

contrast collar and revers

long collar

tight sleeves

bound edges

shoulder cape

fitted waist

buttons to waist

buttons to waist

turn-back cuff

leather gloves

contrast check

leather gloves

knee-length coat

cutaway coat

full-skirted coat

fitted trousers

long overcoat

formal evening wear

fine leather boots

contrast toe-caps

'stirrup' under boot

flowers and ribbons

bonnets with shallow crowns and closed brims

feathers and looped ribbon

pleated fabric

wide open brim

decorative edge to brims

dropped shoulderline

embroidered ribbons

puffed oversleeve

buttons

pleated bodice

buckle fastening

high waist positions, narrow belts

leg-of-mutton sleeves

tight undersleeve

turn-down cuffs

elbow-length gloves

tiny bag with ribbon handle

button trim

striped fabric

skirts off the ground, frilled hems

flat, low-cut pumps

tall top hats

'M' cut collar

curled hair and side whiskers

high-buttoned waistcoat

shoulder cape

tight sleeves

leather gloves

double-breasted frock coat

straight-cut trousers

leather boots

wide revers

cravat bound high around the neck

double-breasted waistcoat

trouser pockets

matching waistcoat and trousers

check fabrics

collar cut without revers

gathers

tight-fitting coat

pointed waistcoat

coat cut away at the front

ankle-length coat

leather boots with dark toe-caps

hair decorated with ribbons and flowers

pleated silk

hats with wide brims

drop earrings

pearl necklace

three lace collars

ribbon streamers

off the shoulder

shoulder cape

pleated collar

huge puff sleeves

pleated bodice

belt with buckle

fur muff

double cuff

pelisse (long coat)

fine shawl with fringed hem

lace and tucks

wide skirt decorated with frills and flowers

lace decoration

silk boots with tiny heels

flat silk pumps

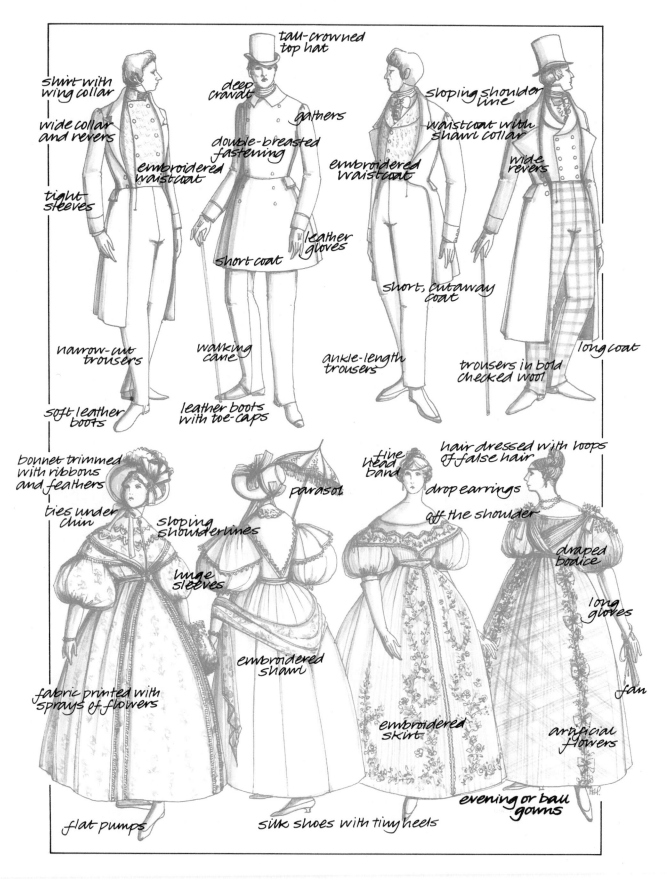

shirt with wing collar

wide collar and revers

embroidered waistcoat

tight sleeves

narrow-cut trousers

soft leather boots

tall-crowned top hat

deep cravat

gathers

double-breasted fastening

short coat

leather gloves

walking cane

leather boots with toe-caps

sloping shoulder line

waistcoat with shawl collar

embroidered waistcoat

short, cutaway coat

ankle-length trousers

wide revers

long coat

trousers in bold checked wool

bonnet trimmed with ribbons and feathers

ties under chin

sloping shoulderlines

huge sleeves

fabric printed with sprays of flowers

flat pumps

parasol

embroidered shawl

silk shoes with tiny heels

fine head band

drop earrings

off the shoulder

embroidered skirt

hair dressed with loops of false hair

draped bodice

long gloves

fan

artificial flowers

evening or ball gowns

frilled edge to shirt

bow tie

waistcoat with shawl collar

revers faced in contrast fabric

contrast collar and revers

low-cut waistcoat

gathered sleeve head

flap pockets

tight-fitting sleeves

set-in cuffs

knee-length frock coat

pleated detail

open vent

long jackets cut away at the front

'stirrup' under foot

narrow trousers

evening suits

boots with long tapering front

bonnets trimmed with ribbons and feathers

tied with ribbons under the chin

small, close-fitting bonnets

tiered shoulder cape

off the shoulder lace collar

deep collar

embroidery

tiered collar with scalloped edge

huge sleeves

waist belts

narrow peplum

natural waist position

belt at high waist position

fur muff

embroidered bag

decorative hem

tiered skirt with scalloped and embroidered edges

skirt off the ground

fine leather or silk boots

skirts touch the ground

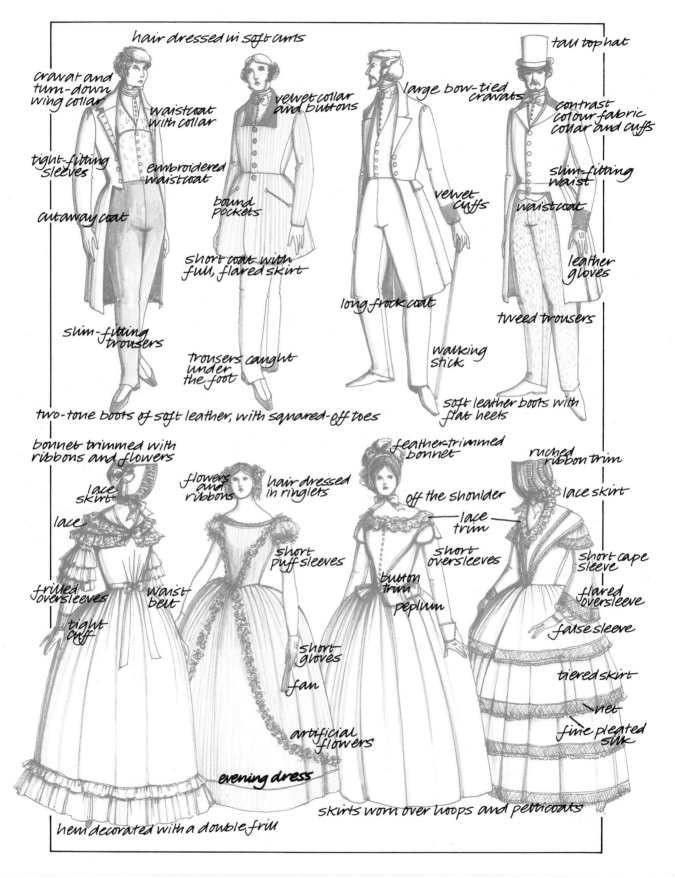

hair dressed in soft curls

tall top hat

cravat and turn-down wing collar

waistcoat with collar

velvet collar and buttons

large bow-tied cravats

contrast colour fabric collar and cuffs

tight-fitting sleeves

embroidered waistcoat

slim-fitting waist

cutaway coat

bound pockets

velvet cuffs

waistcoat

short coat with full, flared skirt

leather gloves

slim-fitting trousers

trousers caught under the foot

long frock coat

walking stick

tweed trousers

soft leather boots with flat heels

two-tone boots of soft leather, with squared-off toes

bonnet trimmed with ribbons and flowers

feather-trimmed bonnet

ruched ribbon trim

lace skirt

flowers and ribbons

hair dressed in ringlets

off the shoulder

lace skirt

lace

lace trim

short oversleeves

short cape sleeve

frilled oversleeves

waist belt

short puff sleeves

button trim

peplum

flared oversleeve

false sleeve

tight cuff

short gloves

tiered skirt

fan

net

artificial flowers

fine pleated silk

evening dress

skirts worn over hoops and petticoats

hem decorated with a double frill

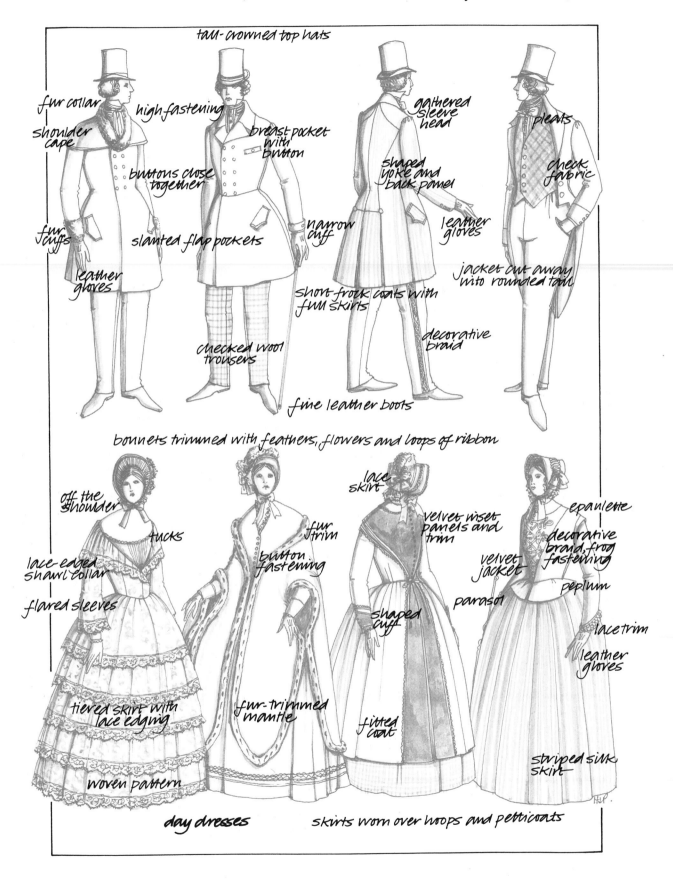

tall-crowned top hats

fur collar

high fastening

shoulder cape

breast pocket with button

gathered sleeve head

pleats

buttons close together

shaped yoke and back panel

check fabric

fur cuffs

narrow cuff

leather gloves

slanted flap pockets

leather gloves

jacket cut away into rounded tail

short frock coats with full skirts

checked wool trousers

decorative braid

fine leather boots

bonnets trimmed with feathers, flowers and loops of ribbon

off the shoulder

tucks

lace skirt

velvet inset panels and trim

epaulette

lace-edged shawl collar

fur trim

button fastening

decorative braid, frog fastening

velvet jacket

flared sleeves

shaped cuff

parasol

peplum

lace trim

leather gloves

tiered skirt with lace edging

fur-trimmed mantle

fitted coat

striped silk skirt

woven pattern

day dresses

skirts worn over hoops and petticoats

hair dressed in curls over the ears

high stand collar

dark bow tie

shawl collar

deep revers

button holes

double-breasted waistcoat

flap pockets

buttons

coat with full, flared skirt

boldly checked trousers

full trousers with narrow hem

striped fabric

leather boots

top hats with curled brims

braid trim

breast pocket with silk hankie

seamed cuff

cutaway coat

cutaway coat

short cloak

gloves

walking cane

evening suit and short cape

bonnets trimmed with feathers, flowers and ribbons

small bonnet

fur collar

buttoned jacket

button trim (back fastening)

lace trim

posy of flowers

lace frill

peplum

short oversleeves

tight sleeves

fine cashmere shawl

bow trim

fur trim

fur muff

fine silk mantle

leather gloves

bodice cut as a jacket

deep fringing

lace and frilled trim

covered buttons

draped silk

fur-trimmed skirt

skirt cut in tiers, worn over a crinoline and petticoat

skirt trimmed with bands of lace

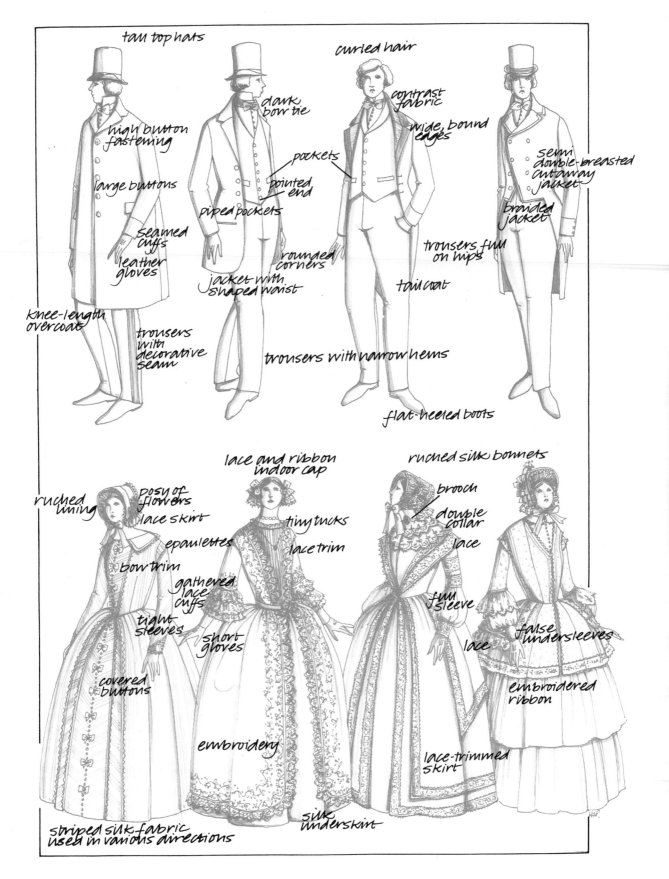

tall top hats

curled hair

high button fastening

dark bow tie

contrast fabric

wide, bound edges

large buttons

pockets

pointed end

semi double-breasted cutaway jacket

piped pockets

seamed cuffs

leather gloves

jacket with shaped waist

rounded corners

braided jacket

trousers full on hips

tail coat

knee-length overcoat

trousers with decorative seam

trousers with narrow hems

flat-heeled boots

lace and ribbon indoor cap

ruched silk bonnets

ruched lining

posy of flowers

lace skirt

epaulettes

tiny tucks

brooch

double collar

lace

bow trim

lace trim

gathered lace cuffs

tight sleeves

short gloves

full sleeve

lace

false undersleeves

covered buttons

embroidered ribbon

embroidery

lace-trimmed skirt

striped silk fabric used in various directions

silk underskirt

tall-crowned top hats

curled hair

curled hair

side whiskers and moustaches

bow tie and wing collar

waist coat with collar

large collar and revers

large check

button holes

set of four-flap pockets

double-breasted jacket

braided edges

flap pockets

tucks

buttons

long waistcoat

sewn cuffs

trousers with fly-front fastening

low-set pockets

leather gloves

cutaway coat

straight-cut trousers

long frock coat

soft leather boots

leather boots with flat heels

hair dressed flat to the head, with a small back bun and side ringlets

shallow bonnet trimmed with ribbon

peter pan collar

tucks

ribbons and flowers

feather trim

lace skirt

fringe

tiered lace frills

large collar and revers

puff sleeves

long gloves

fringing

low point to bodice

lace

false sleeves

embroidered jacket

striped silk dress decorated with velvet ribbons and fringing

riding costume

tiered skirt trimmed with lace and embroidery

travelling costume

fabric cap with hard peak

large bow tie

collar

collar and revers

contrast fabric and colour on collar and revers

striped fabric

four pockets in waistcoat

waistcoat with high fastening

bias-cut waistcoat

pocket on waist

seamed cuff

contrast fabric and colour

short jacket

curved edge

frock coat hems above knee level

braided edges

check trousers

silk parasol trimmed with ribbons

ribbons and flowers

fringe

embroidery

flowers

lace collars

long gloves

velvet jacket

embroidered ribbon

lace

short gloves

muslin skirt and sleeves, pointed edges

posies of flowers and ribbons

folding fan

striped muslin skirt trimmed with ribbons

tiered overskirt of lace

evening gown
trimmed with frills, ribbon, ruching, embroidery, lace, and silk flowers

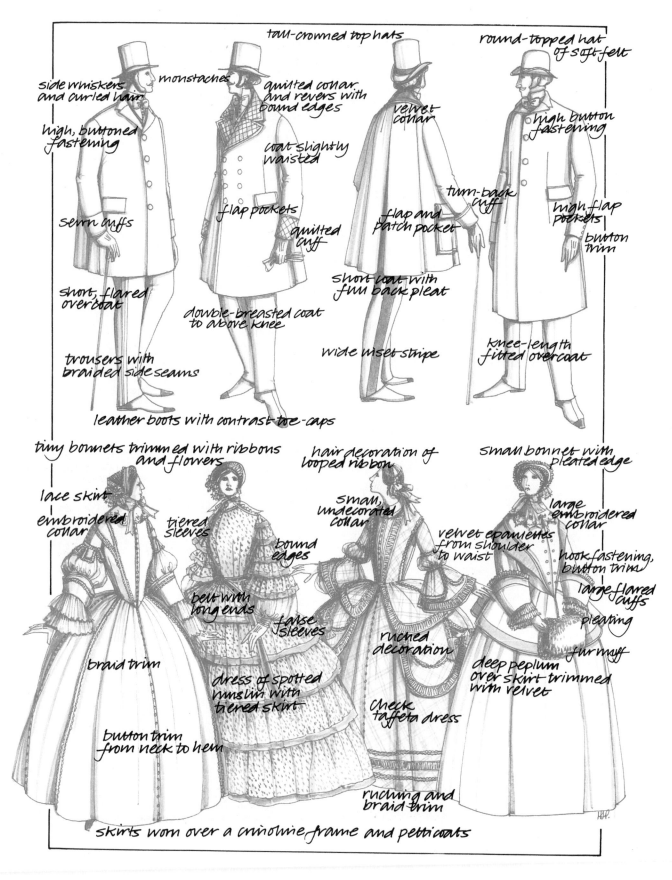

tall-crowned top hats

round-topped hat of soft felt

side whiskers and curled hair

monstaches

quilted collar and revers with bound edges

velvet collar

high button fastening

high, buttoned fastening

coat slightly waisted

turn-back cuff

high flap pockets

sewn cuffs

flap pockets

flap and patch pocket

button trim

quilted cuff

short, flared overcoat

short coat with full back pleat

double-breasted coat to above knee

knee-length fitted overcoat

trousers with braided side seams

wide inset stripe

leather boots with contrast toe-caps

tiny bonnets trimmed with ribbons and flowers

hair decoration of looped ribbon

small bonnet with pleated edge

lace skirt

small, undecorated collar

embroidered collar

tiered sleeves

bound edges

velvet epaulettes from shoulder to waist

large embroidered collar

hook fastening, button trim

belt with long ends

false sleeves

large flared cuffs

braid trim

ruched decoration

pleating

fur muff

dress of spotted muslin with tiered skirt

deep peplum over skirt trimmed with velvet

button trim from neck to hem

check taffeta dress

ruching and braid trim

HP.

skirts worn over a crinoline frame and petticoats

round-topped hat of soft felt

low-cut waistcoat

four pockets

long casual jacket

breast pocket

patch pockets

straight-cut trousers

curled hair and long side whiskers, with moustaches

dark silk collar and revers

cutaway jacket

fitted waistcoat with collar

pocket in side seam

evening suit

boots with dark toe-caps

soft-felt bowler hats

high button fastening

braided edges

breast pocket

double-breasted waistcoat

fitted jacket

flap pockets

leather gloves

walking cane

striped trousers

covered buttons

long double-breasted jacket

felt spats over boots

small bonnet trimmed with lace and loops of ribbon

plaited and coiled hair

tiered sleeve

flared oversleeve

buttoned front

false sleeve into tight cuff

tiered skirt with embroidered binding

small bonnet with ruching inside brim

tiny silk flowers

collar

cape

belt with bow and long streamers

tiers cut into points with lace edging

striped taffeta dress

hair decorated with ribbons and flowers

large brooch

back hair held in a net

bias-cut bindings

buttons

pockets

velvet travelling coat with contrast colour velvet trim

decorative strap and button fastenings

floating panels

bound hem

bowler hat

top hats with wide bands

shallow bowler

knotted tie

high fastenings

turn-down collar with knotted tie

wool tweed

pocket handkerchief

turn-back cuff

flap pocket

low seam

cuffs

buttoned cuffs

bound pockets

flap pockets

hip-length jacket

knee-length overcoat

flared overcoat

check trousers

narrow trousers

walking cane

leather boots

contrast toe-caps and heels

leather boots with dark suede toe-caps

shallow bonnets

tiny pill-box hat trimmed with feathers

hair decoration of ribbons and flowers

flower and ribbon trim

lace trim

hair worn in braids and loops

drop earrings

lace skirt

drop shoulderline

braid decoration

wide neckline

striped silk

fur

embroidery

wide, flared sleeves

applied ribbon

fringe and tassel trim

false undersleeves

jacket fastened at the waist

wide, flared sleeves

frilled and ruched decoration

silk with woven flower design

ribbon and braid hem detail

skirts with short trains worn over oval-shaped hoops

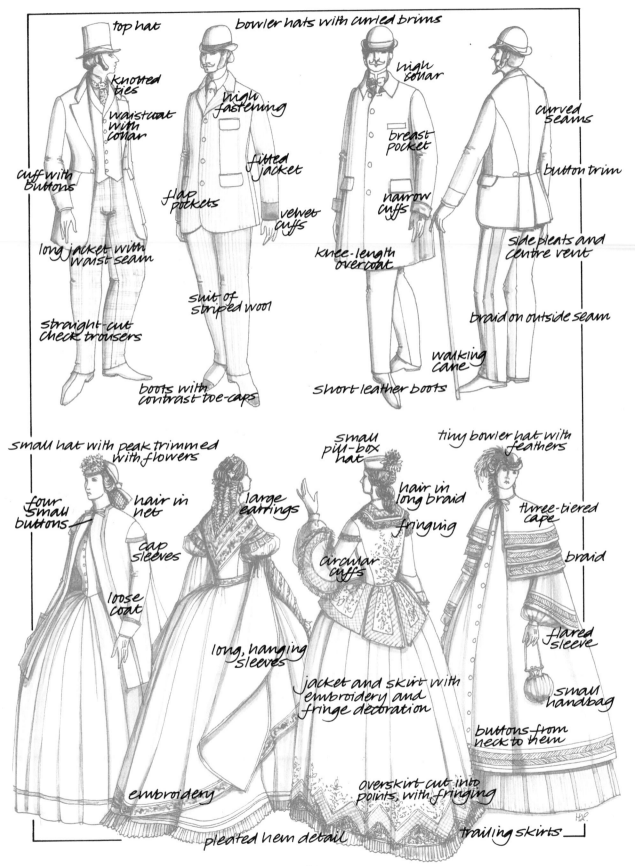

top hat

bowler hats with curled brims

knotted ties

high fastening

high collar

waistcoat with collar

breast pocket

curved seams

cuff with buttons

fitted jacket

button trim

flap pockets

velvet cuffs

narrow cuffs

long jacket with waist seam

knee-length overcoat

side pleats and centre vent

braid on outside seam

straight-cut check trousers

suit of striped wool

walking cane

boots with contrast toe-caps

short leather boots

small hat with peak trimmed with flowers

small pill-box hat

tiny bowler hat with feathers

four small buttons

hair in net

large earrings

hair in long braid

three-tiered cape

cap sleeves

fringing

braid

loose coat

circular cuffs

long, hanging sleeves

flared sleeve

jacket and skirt with embroidery and fringe decoration

small handbag

buttons from neck to hem

embroidery

overskirt cut into points, with fringing

pleated hem detail

trailing skirts

fur overcollar

collar

breast pocket

covered buttons

cuff

fur overcuff

leather gloves

long coat of heavy wool tweed

silk-trimmed collar and revers

frilled shirt

double-breasted waistcoat

silk-faced cuff

silk braid

evening suit

small bowler hat

astrakhan collar and trim

braid and button fastenings

short casual or sports jacket

leather ankle boots

high stand collar

high button fastening

flap pockets

braided edges

leather gloves

walking cane

small bonnet

hair in net

velvet collar and trim

travelling jacket and skirt of fine wool with velvet trim

pleated hem on underskirt

hair coiled high on head

short gloves

cap sleeves

back ringlets

bows

puff sleeves

lace

slightly high waist position

pads and frilled petticoats

tiny hats decorated with ribbons and flowers

ruched trim

striped silk

skirts drawn back in swags to form trains

back veil

fringing

high waist position

velvet ribbon and fringing

H.P.

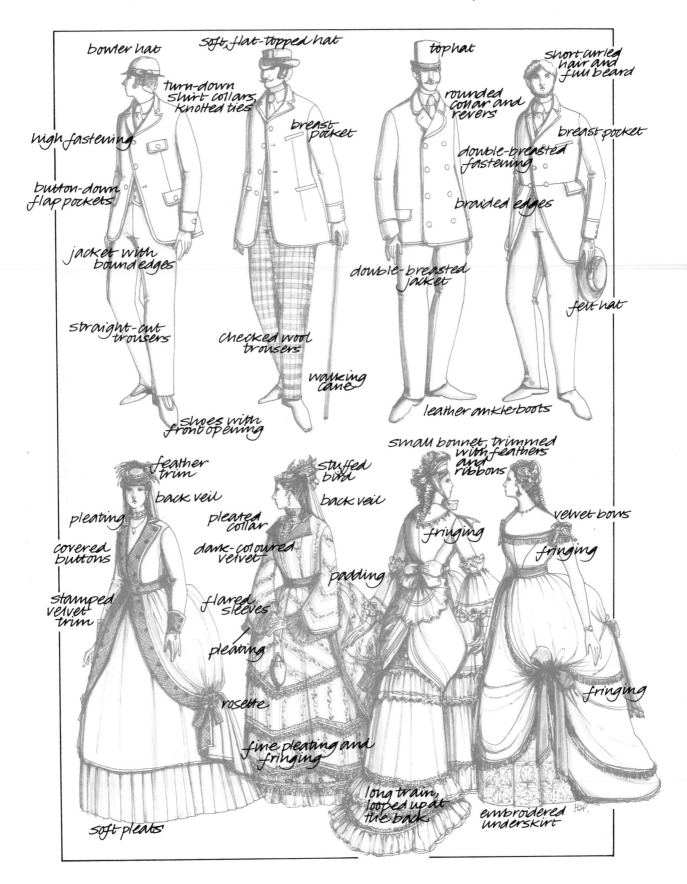

bowler hat

soft, flat-topped hat

tophat

short curled hair and full beard

turn-down shirt collars, knotted ties

breast pocket

rounded collar and revers

breast pocket

high fastening

double-breasted fastening

button-down flap pockets

braided edges

jacket with bound edges

double-breasted jacket

felt hat

straight-cut trousers

checked wool trousers

walking cane

leather ankle-boots

shoes with front opening

feather trim

stuffed bird

small bonnet, trimmed with feathers and ribbons

back veil

back veil

velvet bows

pleating

pleated collar

fringing

covered buttons

dark-coloured velvet

padding

fringing

stamped velvet trim

flared sleeves

pleating

rosette

fine pleating and fringing

fringing

soft pleats

long train, looped up at the back

embroidered underskirt

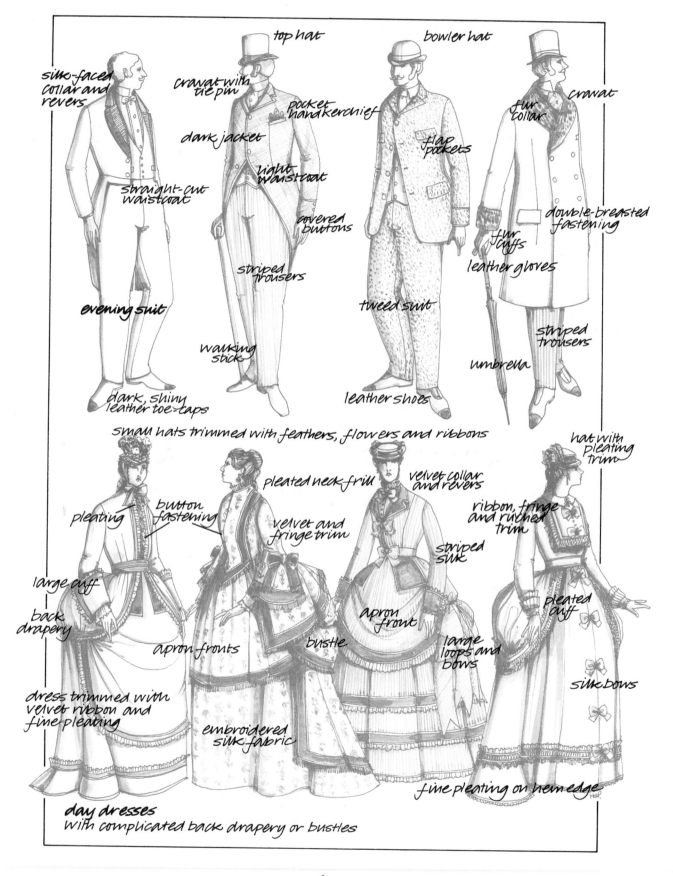

silk-faced collar and revers

top hat

cravat with tie pin

pocket handkerchief

dark jacket

light waistcoat

straight-cut waistcoat

covered buttons

striped trousers

evening suit

walking sticks

dark, shiny leather toe-taps

bowler hat

flap pockets

tweed suit

leather shoes

fur collar

cravat

double-breasted fastening

fur cuffs

leather gloves

striped trousers

umbrella

small hats trimmed with feathers, flowers and ribbons

pleating

button fastening

pleated neck frill

velvet and fringe trim

velvet collar and revers

hat with pleating trim

ribbon, fringe and ruched trim

striped silk

large cuff

back drapery

apron fronts

bustle

apron front

large loops and bows

pleated cuff

silk bows

dress trimmed with velvet ribbon and fine pleating

embroidered silk fabric

fine pleating on hem edge

day dresses
with complicated back drapery or bustles

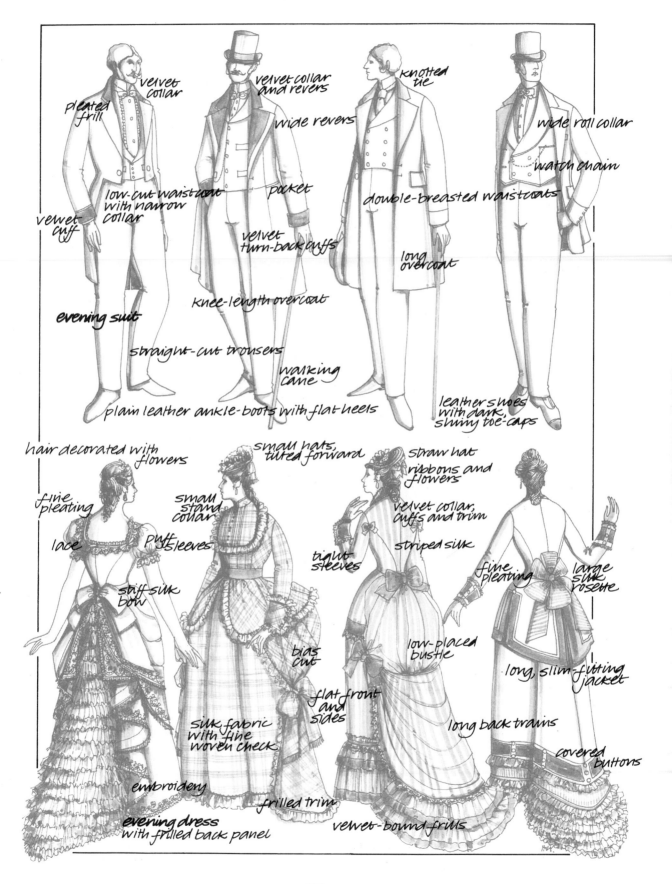

velvet collar

pleated frill

velvet cuff

low-cut waistcoat with narrow collar

evening suit

velvet collar and revers

wide revers

pocket

velvet turn-back cuffs

knee-length overcoat

straight-cut trousers

walking cane

plain leather ankle-boots with flat heels

knotted tie

double-breasted waistcoats

long overcoat

wide roll collar

watch chain

leather shoes with dark, shiny toe-caps

hair decorated with flowers

fine pleating

lace

puff sleeves

stiff silk bow

embroidery

evening dress with frilled back panel

small hats, tilted forward

small stand collar

silk fabric with fine woven check

bias cut

flat front and sides

frilled trim

straw hat

ribbons and flowers

velvet collar, cuffs and trim

striped silk

tight sleeves

low-placed bustle

velvet-bound frills

fine pleating

large silk rosette

long, slim-fitting jacket

long back trains

covered buttons

VICTORIA · 1837~1901 (viii) C.1875~80

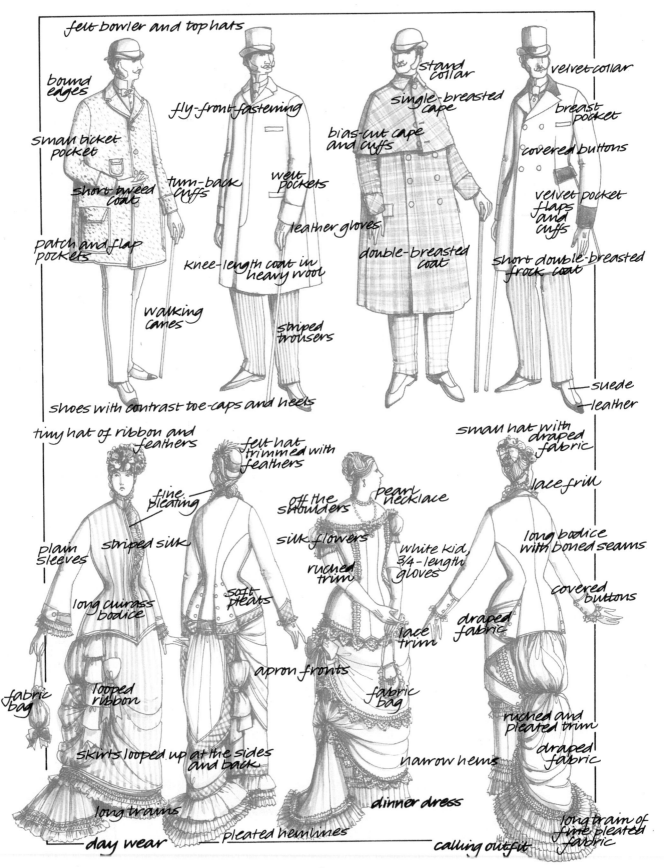

felt bowler and top hats

bound edges

small ticket pocket

short tweed coat

patch and flap pockets

fly-front fastening

turn-back cuffs

welt pockets

leather gloves

knee-length coat in heavy wool

walking canes

striped trousers

stand collar

single-breasted cape

bias-cut cape and cuffs

double-breasted coat

velvet collar

breast pocket

covered buttons

velvet pocket flaps and cuffs

short double-breasted frock coat

suede

leather

shoes with contrast toe-caps and heels

tiny hat of ribbon and feathers

fine pleating

plain sleeves

striped silk

long cuirass bodice

fabric bag

looped ribbon

skirts looped up at the sides and back

long trains

day wear

felt hat trimmed with feathers

soft pleats

apron fronts

pleated hemlines

off the shoulders

silk flowers

ruched trim

lace trim

fabric bag

dinner dress

pearl necklace

white kid, 3/4-length gloves

narrow hems

small hat with draped fabric

lace frill

long bodice with boned seams

covered buttons

draped fabric

ruched and pleated trim

draped fabric

long train of fine pleated fabric

calling outfit

98

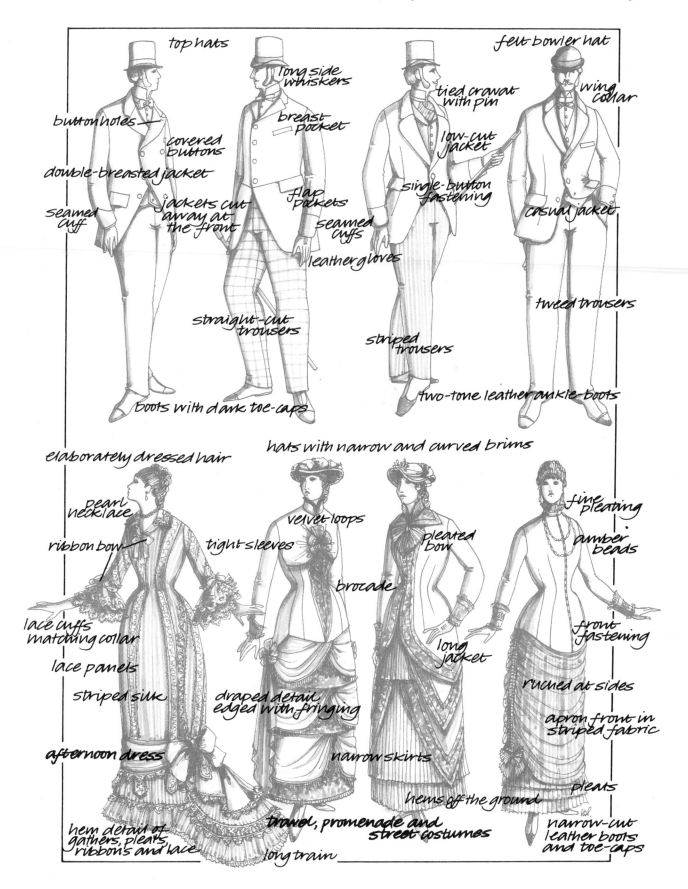

top hats

felt bowler hat

button holes

long side whiskers

tied cravat with pin

wing collar

covered buttons

breast pocket

low-cut jacket

double-breasted jacket

single-button fastening

casual jacket

seamed cuff

jackets cut away at the front

flap pockets

seamed cuffs

leather gloves

tweed trousers

straight-cut trousers

striped trousers

boots with dark toe-caps

two-tone leather ankle-boots

elaborately dressed hair

hats with narrow and curved brims

pearl necklace

velvet loops

pleated bow

fine pleating

ribbon bow

tight sleeves

amber beads

brocade

long jacket

lace cuffs matching collar

front fastening

lace panels

draped detail edged with fringing

ruched at sides

striped silk

apron front in striped fabric

afternoon dress

narrow skirts

hems off the ground

pleats

hem detail of gathers, pleats, ribbons and lace

travel, promenade and street costumes

narrow-cut leather boots and toe-caps

long train

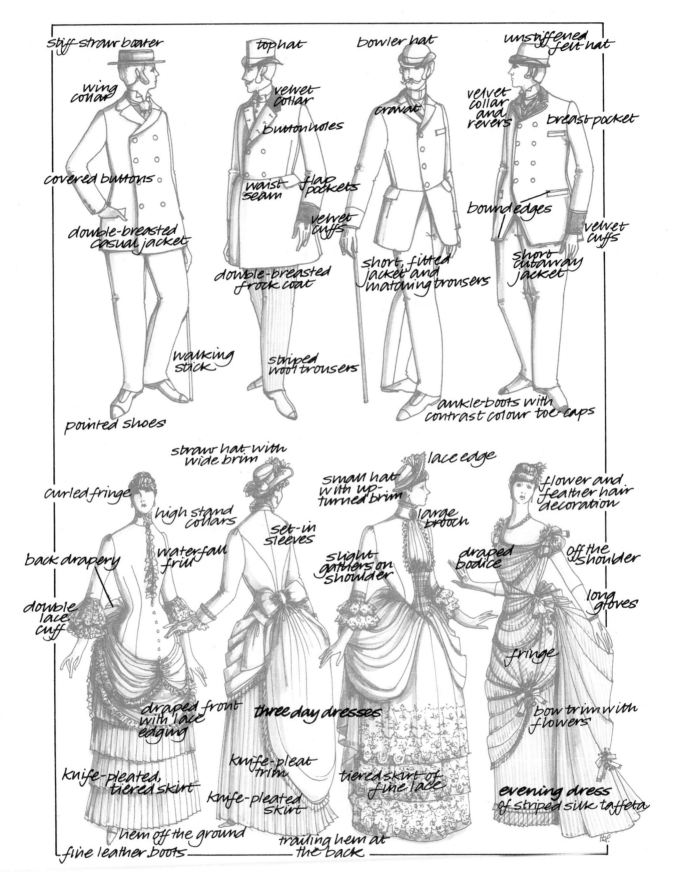

stiff straw boater

wing collar

covered buttons

double-breasted casual jacket

walking stick

pointed shoes

top hat

velvet collar

buttonholes

waist seam

flap pockets

velvet cuffs

double-breasted frock coat

striped wool trousers

bowler hat

cravat

short, fitted jacket and matching trousers

ankle-boots with contrast colour toe-caps

unstiffened felt hat

velvet collar and revers

breast pocket

bound edges

velvet cuffs

short cutaway jacket

curled fringe

high stand collars

back drapery

waterfall frill

double lace cuff

draped front with lace edging

knife-pleated, tiered skirt

hem off the ground

fine leather boots

straw hat with wide brim

set-in sleeves

three day dresses

knife-pleat trim

knife-pleated skirt

trailing hem at the back

small hat with up-turned brim

lace edge

large brooch

slight gathers on shoulder

tiered skirt of fine lace

flower and feather hair decoration

draped bodice

off the shoulder

long gloves

fringe

bow trim with flowers

evening dress of striped silk taffeta

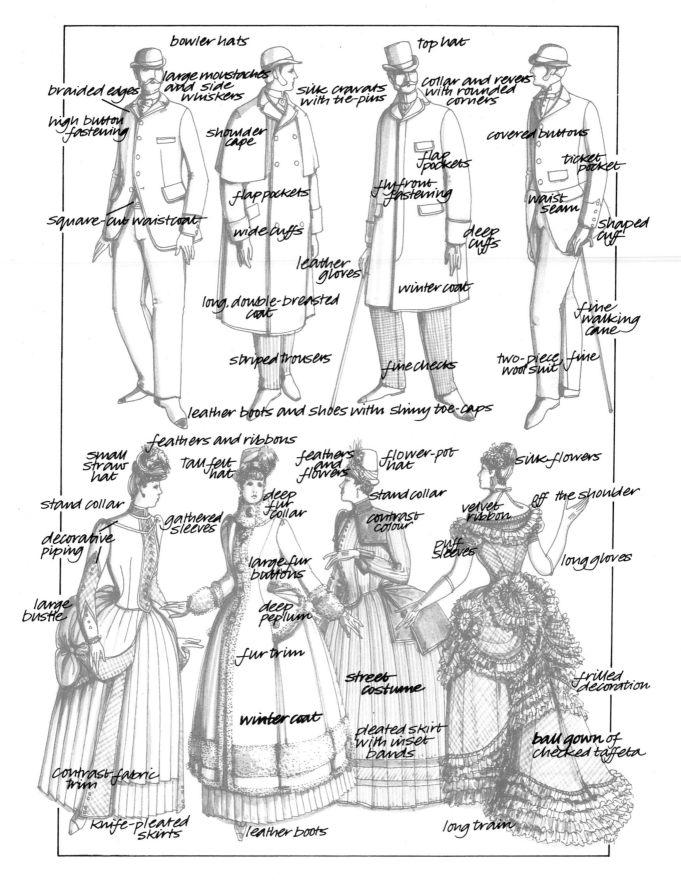

bowler hats

top hat

braided edges

large moustaches and side whiskers

silk cravats with tie-pins

collar and revers with rounded corners

high button fastening

shoulder cape

covered buttons

flap pockets

ticket pocket

fly front fastening

square-cut waistcoat

flap pockets

waist seam

wide cuffs

deep cuffs

shaped cuff

leather gloves

winter coat

long, double-breasted coat

fine walking cane

striped trousers

fine checks

two-piece, fine wool suit

leather boots and shoes with shiny toe-caps

feathers and ribbons

small straw hat

tall felt hat

feathers and flowers

flower-pot hat

silk flowers

stand collar

gathered sleeves

deep fur collar

stand collar

velvet ribbon

off the shoulder

decorative piping

contrast colour

puff sleeves

long gloves

large bustle

large fur buttons

deep peplum

fur trim

frilled decoration

street costume

winter coat

pleated skirt with inset bands

ball gown of checked taffeta

contrast fabric trim

knife-pleated skirts

leather boots

long train

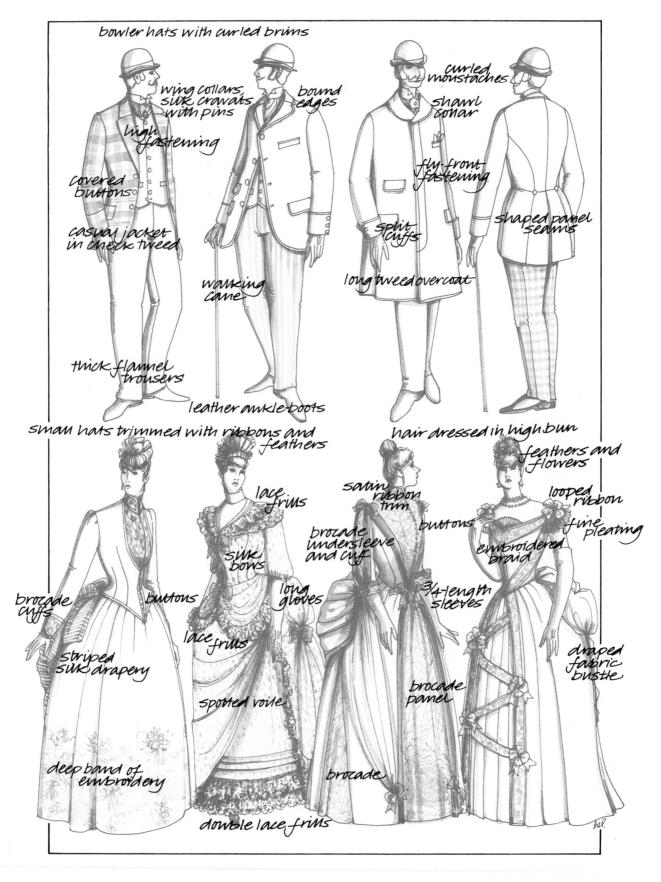

bowler hats with curled brims

wing collars, silk cravats with pins

bound edges

curled moustaches

shawl collar

high fastening

covered buttons

casual jacket in check tweed

fly-front fastening

split cuffs

shaped panel seams

long tweed overcoat

walking cane

thick flannel trousers

leather ankle-boots

small hats trimmed with ribbons and feathers

hair dressed in high bun

feathers and flowers

lace frills

satin ribbon trim

buttons

looped ribbon

brocade undersleeve and cuff

fine pleating

silk bows

embroidered braid

brocade cuffs

buttons

long gloves

3/4-length sleeves

striped silk drapery

lace frills

draped fabric bustle

spotted voile

brocade panel

deep band of embroidery

brocade

double lace frills

wing collars
cravat
high fastening
ticket pocket
knee-length overcoat
leather ankle-boots

bound edges
covered buttons
seam
inset pocket
double-breasted frock coat

bowler hat
knotted ties with pins
flap pockets
casual jacket
check wool trousers

velvet collar and revers
velvet cuffs
frock coat with flared skirt

hair in a bun, with curled fringe
gathers
high stand collar
velvet
silk flowers
stiff belt
heavy silk, woven stripes
pleated panel

pearls
draped chiffon
boned bodice
long kid gloves
apron front with frilled edges
tassels

hat trimmed with feathers and ribbons
wide shoulders
long cuffs
skirts worn over bustle pads and flared petticoats
embroidery and ribbon work

silk flowers
low, square neckline
pleated puff sleeves
draped bodice
long kid gloves
embroidered flowers
large fan
embroidered panel
knife pleats

felt hat with curled brim

wing collars

neck ties

top hats

cravat and pin

high fastening

wide revers

flap pockets

check waistcoat

long overcape

stitching

split cuff

large flap and patch pockets

walking cane with silver knob

slanted flap pockets

knee-length frock coat

flared overcoat

long coat

umbrella

spats

leather ankle-boots with fabric spats

straw hat with large brim

ribbons

fur trim

large hat with feathers

ruched fabric

high stand collars

blouse

blouse

striped silk

lace trim

leg-of-mutton sleeves

gathers

tiny waists

leg-of-mutton sleeves

narrow belts

cut felt and braid

long jacket

flared skirt and silk blouse

skirt, top and blouse

jacket and matching skirt

umbrella

walking costume

small knife pleats

stitching trim

knife-pleated underskirt

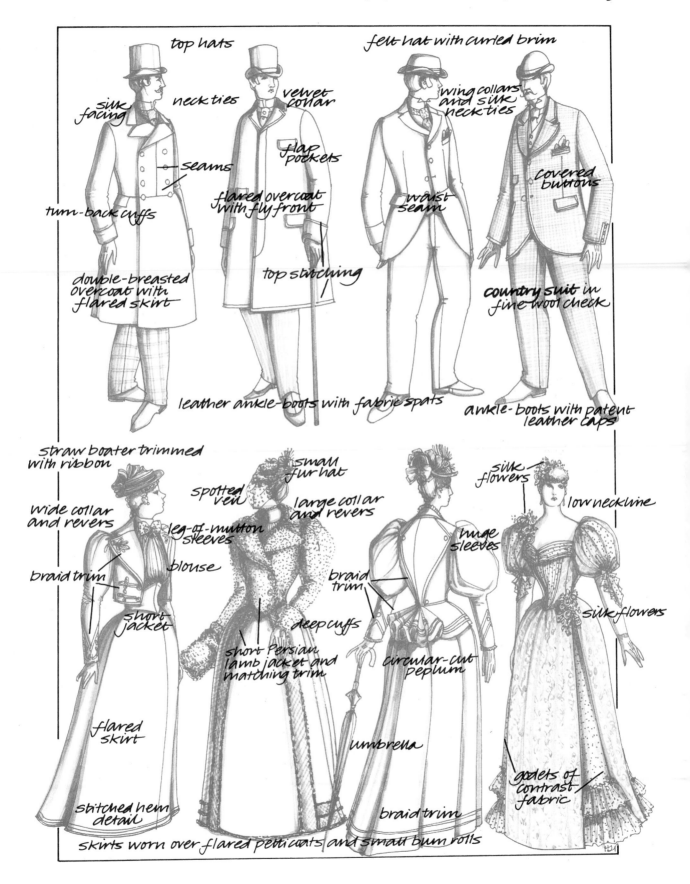

top hats

felt hat with curled brim

silk facing

neck ties

velvet collar

wing collars and silk neckties

seams

flap pockets

covered buttons

turn-back cuffs

flared overcoat with fly front

waist seam

double-breasted overcoat with flared skirt

top stitching

country suit in fine wool check

leather ankle-boots with fabric spats

ankle-boots with patent leather caps

straw boater trimmed with ribbon

small fur hat

silk flowers

wide collar and revers

spotted veil

large collar and revers

low neckline

braid trim

leg-of-mutton sleeves

blouse

braid trim

huge sleeves

short jacket

deep cuffs

short Persian lamb jacket and matching trim

circular-cut peplum

silk flowers

flared skirt

umbrella

godets of contrast fabric

stitched hem detail

skirts worn over flared petticoats and small bum rolls

braid trim

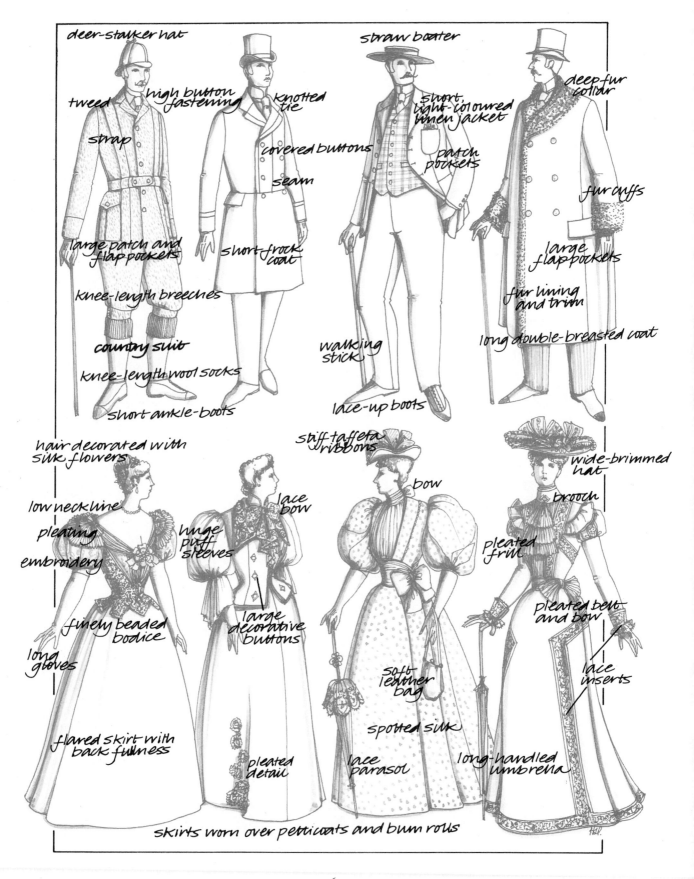

deer-stalker hat

straw boater

deep-fur collar

tweed

high button fastening

knotted tie

short, light-coloured linen jacket

strap

covered buttons

patch pockets

fur cuffs

seam

large patch and flap pockets

short-frock coat

large flap pockets

knee-length breeches

fur lining and trim

country suit

walking stick

long double-breasted coat

knee-length wool socks

short ankle-boots

lace-up boots

hair decorated with silk flowers

stiff taffeta ribbons

bow

wide-brimmed hat

low neckline

lace bow

brooch

pleating

huge puff sleeves

pleated frill

embroidery

finely beaded bodice

large decorative buttons

soft leather bag

pleated belt and bow

long gloves

lace inserts

flared skirt with back fullness

pleated detail

spotted silk

lace parasol

long-handled umbrella

skirts worn over petticoats and bum rolls

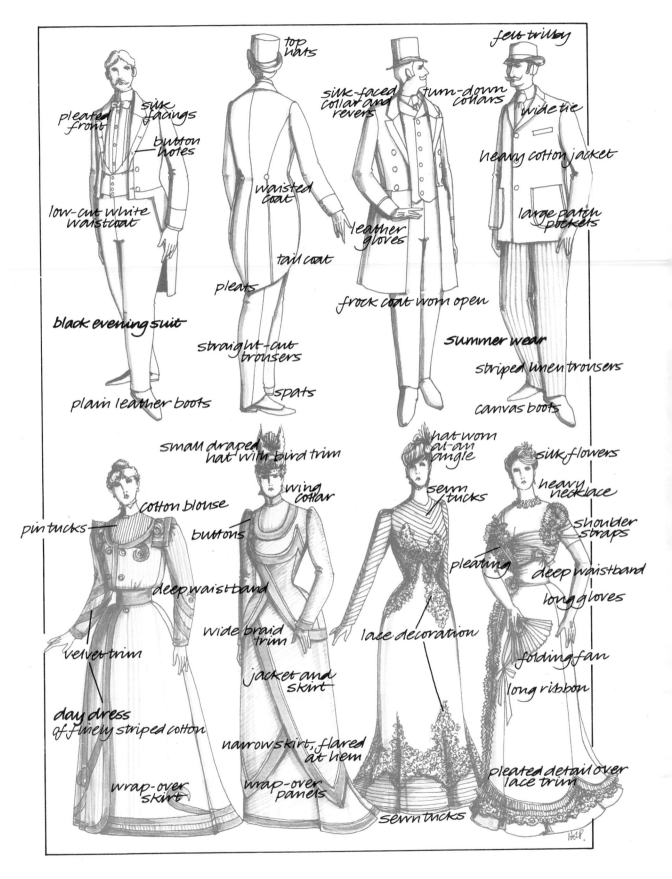

top hats

felt trilby

pleated front

silk facings

button holes

silk-faced collar and revers

turn-down collars

wide tie

low-cut white waistcoat

waisted coat

heavy cotton jacket

large patch pockets

leather gloves

tail coat

black evening suit

pleats

frock coat worn open

summer wear

straight-cut trousers

striped linen trousers

plain leather boots

spats

canvas boots

small draped hat with bird trim

hat worn at an angle

silk flowers

cotton blouse

wing collar

sewn tucks

heavy necklace

pin tucks

buttons

shoulder straps

deep waistband

pleating

deep waistband

long gloves

wide braid trim

lace decoration

velvet trim

jacket and skirt

folding fan

long ribbon

day dress of finely striped cotton

narrow skirt, flared at hem

pleated detail over lace trim

wrap-over skirt

wrap-over panels

sewn tucks

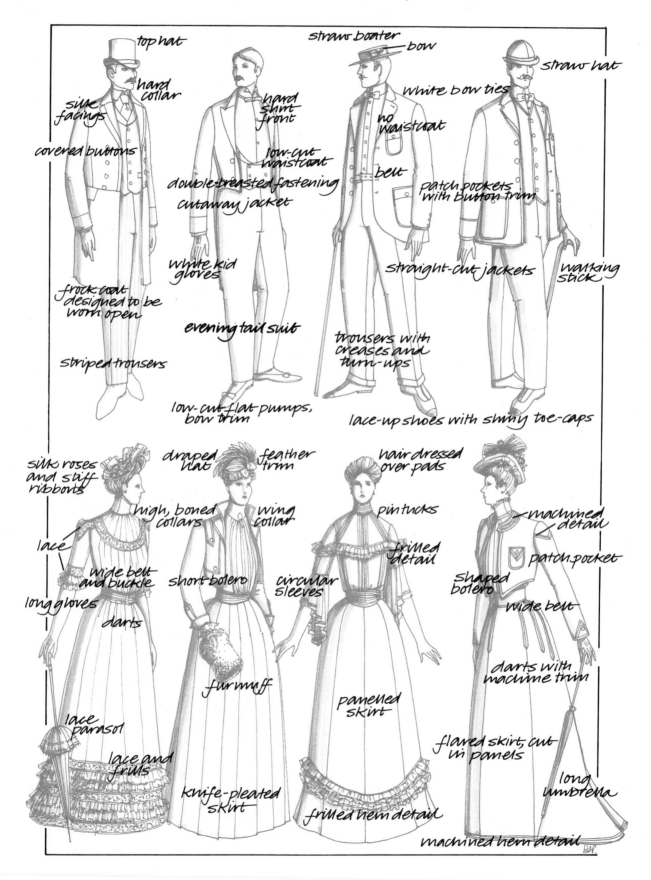

top hat
hard collar
silk facings
covered buttons
frock coat designed to be worn open
striped trousers

straw boater
bow
hard shirt front
low-cut waistcoat
double-breasted fastening
cutaway jacket
white kid gloves
evening tail suit
low-cut flat pumps, bow trim

white bow ties
no waistcoat
belt
patch pockets with button trim
straight-cut jackets
trousers with creases and turn-ups
lace-up shoes with shiny toe-caps

straw hat
walking stick

silk roses and stiff ribbons
lace
high, boned collars
wide belt and buckle
long gloves
darts
lace parasol
lace and frills

draped hat
feather trim
wing collar
short bolero
circular sleeves
fur muff
knife-pleated skirt

hair dressed over pads
pin tucks
frilled detail
panelled skirt
frilled hem detail

machined detail
patch pocket
shaped bolero
wide belt
darts with machine trim
flared skirt, cut in panels
long umbrella
machined hem detail

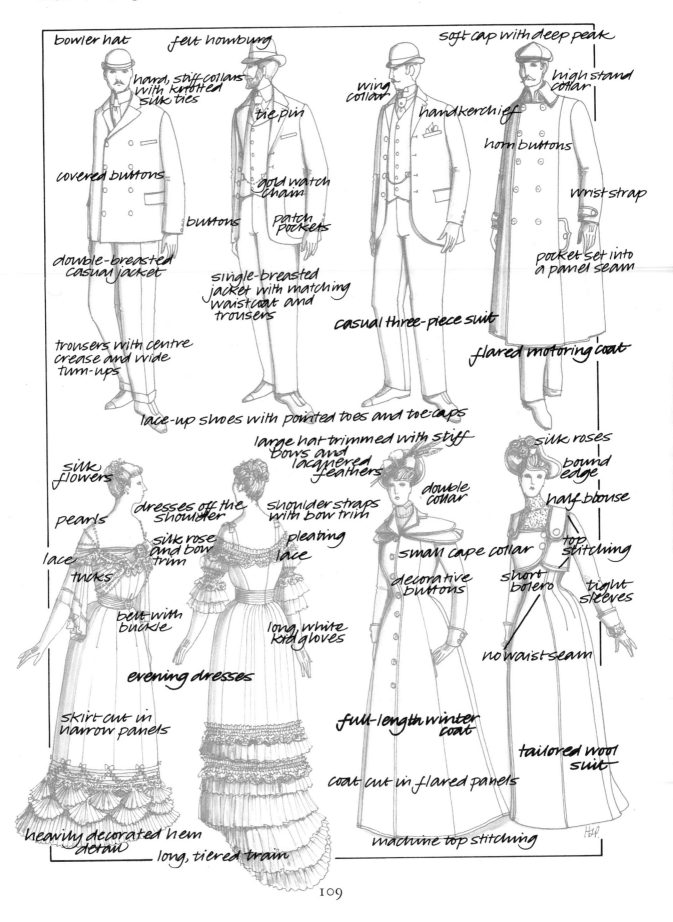

bowler hat

felt homburg

soft cap with deep peak

hard, stiff collars with knotted silk ties

tie pin

wing collar

handkerchief

high stand collar

horn buttons

covered buttons

gold watch chain

wrist strap

buttons

patch pockets

double-breasted casual jacket

single-breasted jacket with matching waistcoat and trousers

pocket set into a panel seam

casual three-piece suit

trousers with centre crease and wide turn-ups

flared motoring coat

lace-up shoes with pointed toes and toe-caps

large hat trimmed with stiff bows and lacquered feathers

silk roses

silk flowers

dresses off the shoulder

shoulder straps with bow trim

double collar

bound edge

pearls

silk rose and bow trim

pleating

half blouse

lace

lace

small cape collar

top stitching

tucks

decorative buttons

short bolero

tight sleeves

belt with buckle

long, white kid gloves

no waist seam

evening dresses

full-length winter coat

skirt cut in narrow panels

tailored wool suit

coat cut in flared panels

heavily decorated hem detail

machine top stitching

long, tiered train

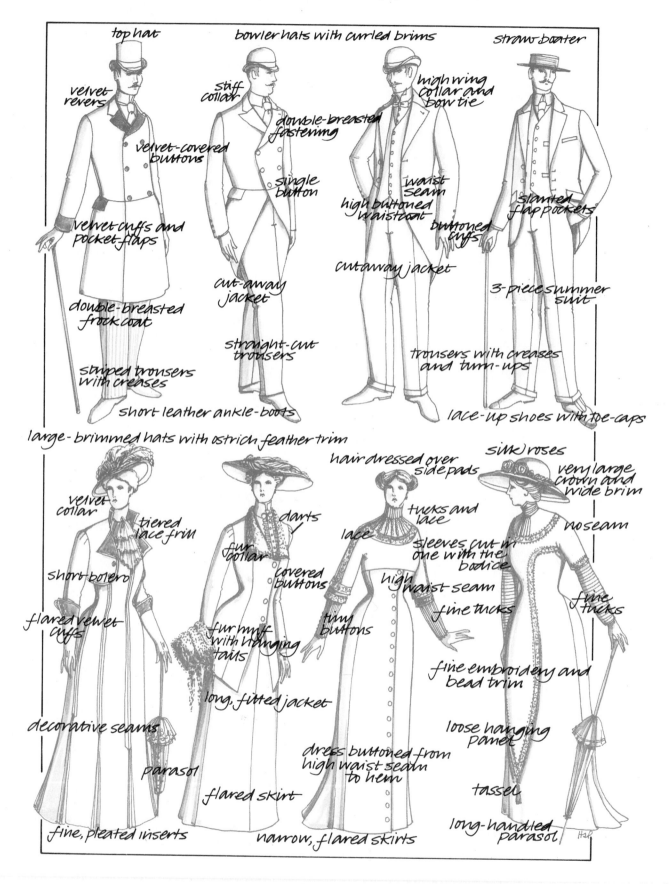

top hat

bowler hats with curled brims

straw boater

velvet revers

velvet-covered buttons

velvet cuffs and pocket-flaps

double-breasted frock coat

striped trousers with creases

stiff collar

double-breasted fastening

single button

cut-away jacket

straight-cut trousers

short leather ankle-boots

high wing collar and bow tie

waist seam

high buttoned waistcoat

buttoned cuffs

cutaway jacket

trousers with creases and turn-ups

slanted flap pockets

3-piece summer suit

lace-up shoes with toe-caps

large-brimmed hats with ostrich feather trim

silk roses

velvet collar

tiered lace frill

short bolero

flared velvet cuffs

decorative seams

parasol

fine, pleated inserts

darts

fur collar

covered buttons

fur muff with hanging tails

long, fitted jacket

flared skirt

narrow, flared skirts

hair dressed over side pads

tucks and lace

lace

sleeves cut in one with the bodice

high waist seam

fine tucks

tiny buttons

dress buttoned from high waist seam to hem

very large crown and wide brim

no seam

fine tucks

fine embroidery and bead trim

loose hanging panel

tassel

long-handled parasol

HₐR

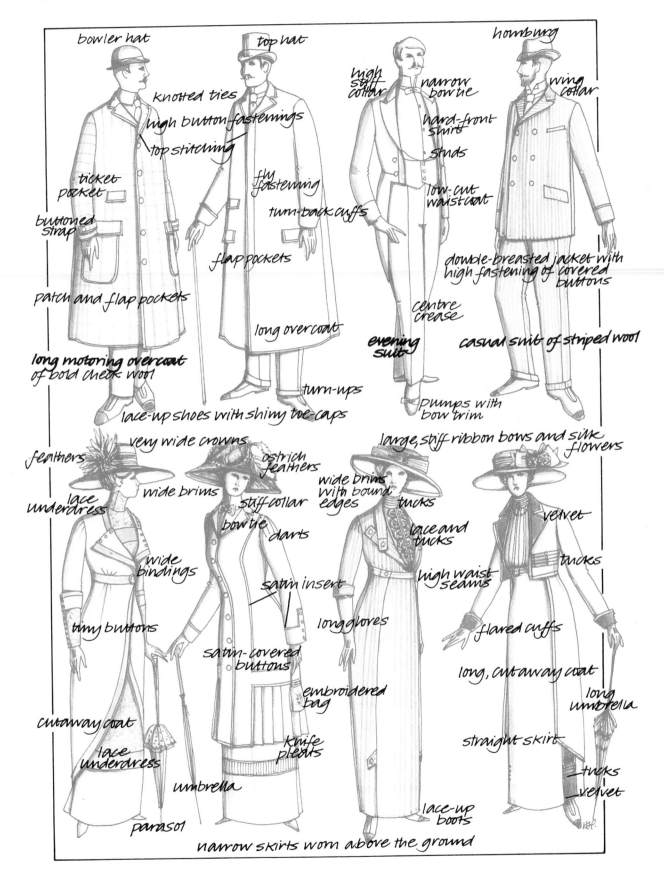

bowler hat

top hat

homburg

knotted ties

high button fastenings

top stitching

ticket pocket

buttoned strap

fly fastening

turn-back cuffs

flap pockets

patch and flap pockets

long overcoat

long motoring overcoat of bold check wool

turn-ups

lace-up shoes with shiny toe-caps

high stiff collar

narrow bow tie

hard-front shirt

studs

low-cut waistcoat

centre crease

evening suit

pumps with bow trim

wing collar

double-breasted jacket with high fastening of covered buttons

casual suit of striped wool

very wide crowns

feathers

lace underdress

wide brims

ostrich feathers

stiff collar

bow tie

darts

wide bindings

satin insert

tiny buttons

satin-covered buttons

embroidered bag

cutaway coat

lace underdress

knife pleats

umbrella

parasol

large, stiff ribbon bows and silk flowers

wide brims with bound edges

tucks

lace and tucks

high waist seams

long gloves

lace-up boots

velvet

tucks

flared cuffs

long, cutaway coat

long umbrella

straight skirt

tucks

velvet

narrow skirts worn above the ground

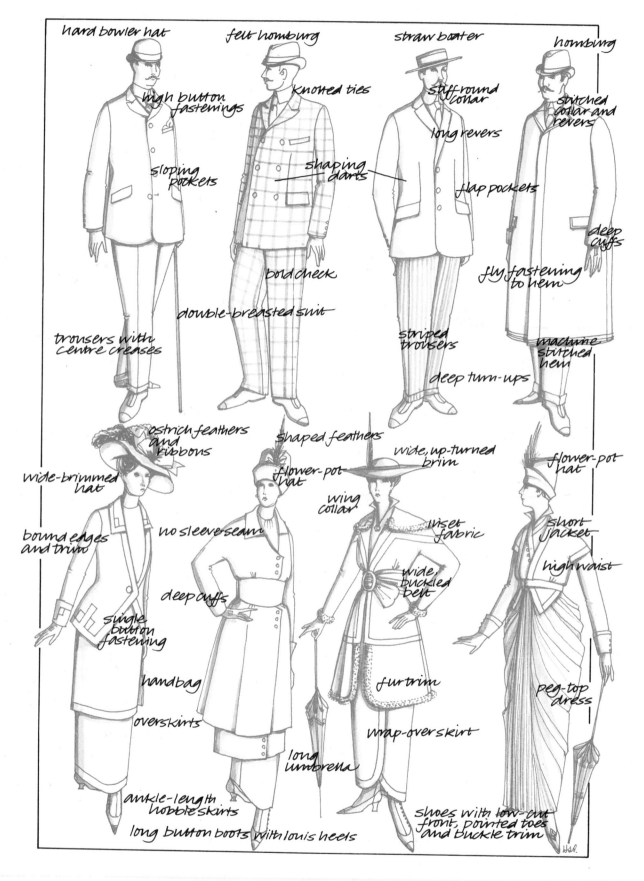

hard bowler hat

felt homburg

straw boater

homburg

high button fastenings

knotted ties

stiff round collar

stitched collar and revers

sloping pockets

long revers

shaping darts

flap pockets

deep cuffs

fly fastening to hem

bold check

double-breasted suit

striped trousers

trousers with centre creases

deep turn-ups

machine stitched hem

ostrich feathers and ribbons

shaped feathers

wide, up-turned brim

flower-pot hat

wide-brimmed hat

flower-pot hat

wing collar

inset fabric

short jacket

bound edges and trim

no sleeve seam

high waist

deep cuffs

wide, buckled belt

single button fastening

handbag

fur trim

peg-top dress

overskirts

wrap-over skirt

long umbrella

ankle-length hobble skirts

shoes with low-cut front, pointed toes and buckle trim

long button boots with louis heels

GEORGE V · 1910~36 (ii) 1916~20

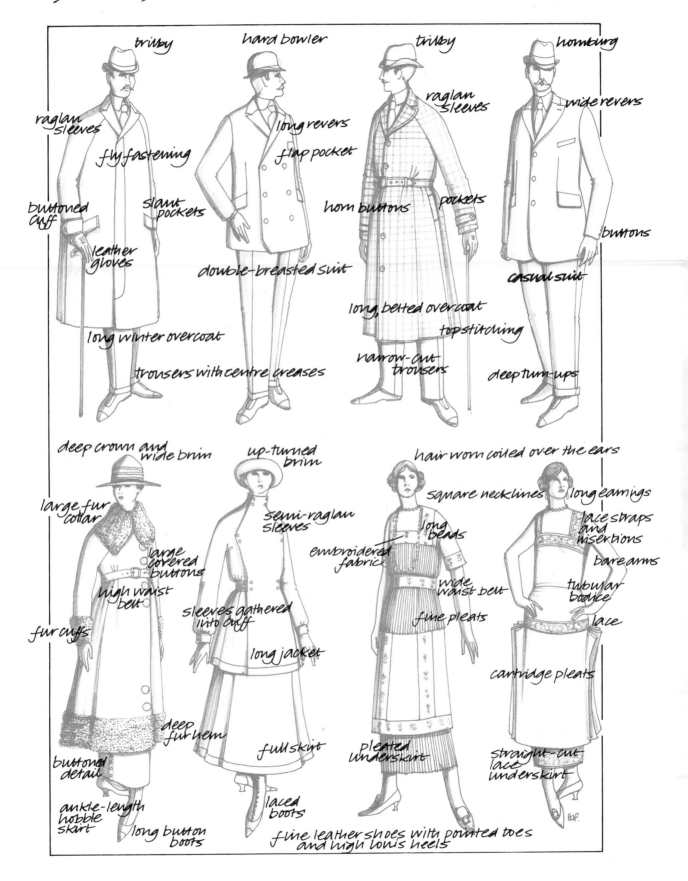

trilby

hard bowler

trilby

homburg

raglan sleeves

fly fastening

long revers

flap pocket

raglan sleeves

wide revers

buttoned cuff

slant pockets

horn buttons

pockets

leather gloves

double-breasted suit

buttons

casual suit

long winter overcoat

long, belted overcoat

topstitching

trousers with centre creases

narrow-cut trousers

deep turn-ups

deep crown and wide brim

up-turned brim

hair worn coiled over the ears

large fur collar

semi-raglan sleeves

square necklines

long earrings

large covered buttons

embroidered fabric

long beads

lace straps and insertions

high waist belt

bare arms

fur cuffs

sleeves gathered into cuff

wide waist belt

tubular bodice

long jacket

fine pleats

lace

cartridge pleats

deep fur hem

full skirt

buttoned detail

pleated underskirt

straight-cut lace underskirt

ankle-length hobble skirt

long button boots

laced boots

fine leather shoes with pointed toes and high Louis heels

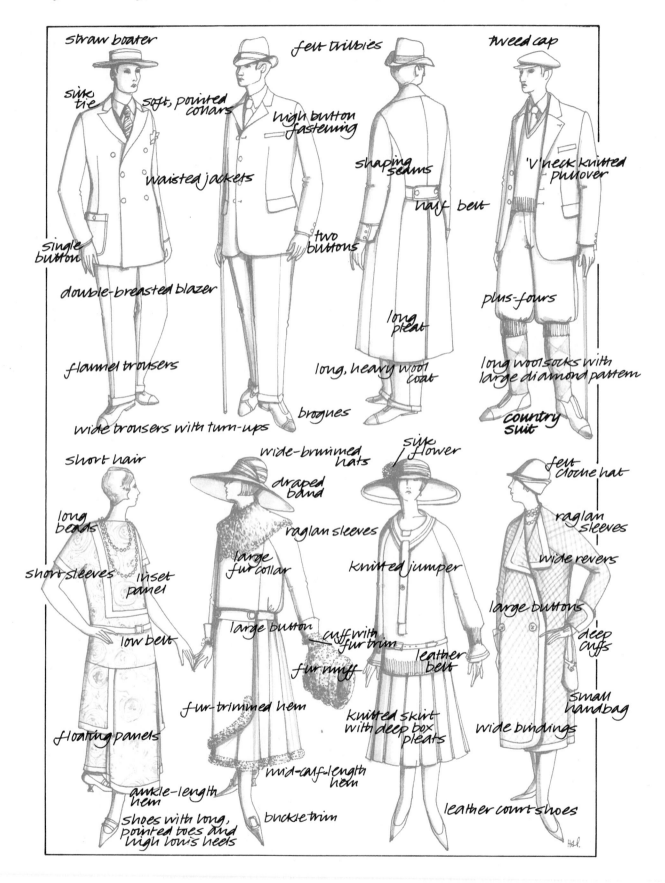

straw boater

felt trilbies

tweed cap

silk tie

soft, pointed collars

high button fastening

waisted jackets

shaping seams

'V'neck knitted pullover

half belt

two buttons

single button

double-breasted blazer

plus-fours

flannel trousers

long pleat

long, heavy wool coat

long wool socks with large diamond pattern

wide trousers with turn-ups

brogues

country suit

short hair

wide-brimmed hats

silk flower

felt cloche hat

long beads

draped band

raglan sleeves

raglan sleeves

short sleeves

inset panel

large fur collar

knitted jumper

wide revers

large buttons

low belt

large button

cuff with fur trim

deep cuffs

fur muff

leather belt

fur-trimmed hem

knitted skirt with deep box pleats

small handbag

floating panels

wide bindings

mid-calf-length hem

ankle-length hem

shoes with long, pointed toes and high louis heels

buckle trim

leather court shoes

trilby

hard bowler

wide, padded shoulders

woolcap

homburg

tie pin through soft collar

silk scarf

silk scarf

breast pocket

horn buttons

double-breasted lounge suit

slanted flap pockets

striped wool

patch pockets

check wool sports jacket

double-breasted coat with flared skirt

coat straight cut to give a narrow hem

wide trousers with turn-ups

wide-cut flannel trousers with turn-ups

brogues

short hair with side parting

wide-brimmed hat

cloche hat

hair cut short

long earrings

stitching

semi-set-in sleeves

glass beads

decorative panels

contrast fabric

fine pleating

leather belt

low belt

long jacket

sequins and beads

point over hand

deep box pleats

fine accordion pleats

fine pleats

knee-length skirts

tubular dress of beaded net over a silk slip

fine silk stockings

silk stockings

leather court shoes with high louis heels

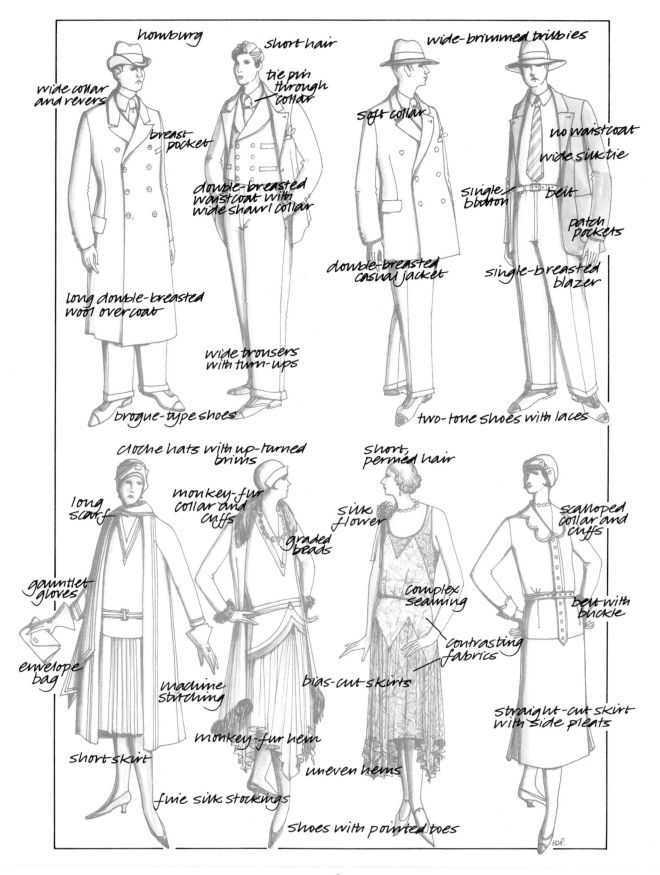

homburg

short hair

wide-brimmed trilbies

wide collar and revers

tie pin through collar

soft collar

no waistcoat

wide silk tie

breast pocket

double-breasted waistcoat with wide shawl collar

single button

belt

patch pockets

double-breasted casual jacket

single-breasted blazer

long double-breasted wool overcoat

wide trousers with turn-ups

brogue-type shoes

two-tone shoes with laces

cloche hats with up-turned brims

short, permed hair

long scarf

monkey-fur collar and cuffs

silk flower

scalloped collar and cuffs

graded beads

gauntlet gloves

complex seaming

belt with buckle

envelope bag

contrasting fabrics

machine stitching

bias-cut skirts

monkey-fur hem

straight-cut skirt with side pleats

short skirt

uneven hems

fine silk stockings

shoes with pointed toes

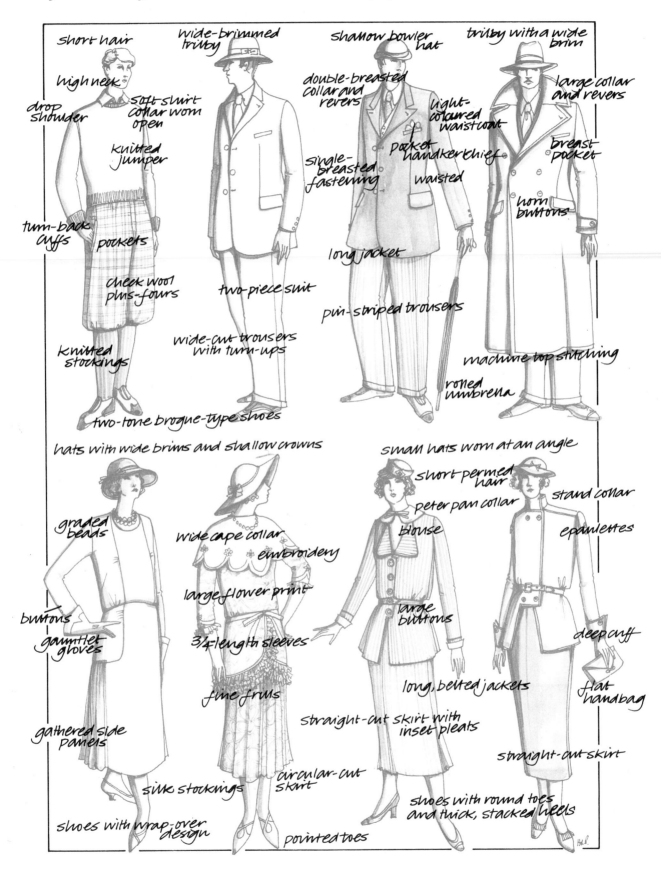

short hair

wide-brimmed trilby

shallow bowler hat

trilby with a wide brim

high neck

double-breasted collar and revers

large collar and revers

drop shoulder

soft shirt collar worn open

light-coloured waistcoat

knitted jumper

pocket handkerchief

breast pocket

single-breasted fastening

waisted

turn-back cuffs

horn buttons

pockets

long jacket

check wool plus-fours

two-piece suit

pin-striped trousers

knitted stockings

wide-cut trousers with turn-ups

machine top stitching

rolled umbrella

two-tone brogue-type shoes

hats with wide brims and shallow crowns

small hats worn at an angle

short permed hair

graded beads

peter pan collar

stand collar

wide cape collar

blouse

epaulettes

embroidery

large flower print

buttons

gauntlet gloves

3/4-length sleeves

large buttons

deep cuff

fine frills

long, belted jackets

flat handbag

gathered side panels

straight-cut skirt with inset pleats

silk stockings

circular-cut skirt

straight-cut skirt

shoes with wrap-over design

pointed toes

shoes with round toes and thick, stacked heels

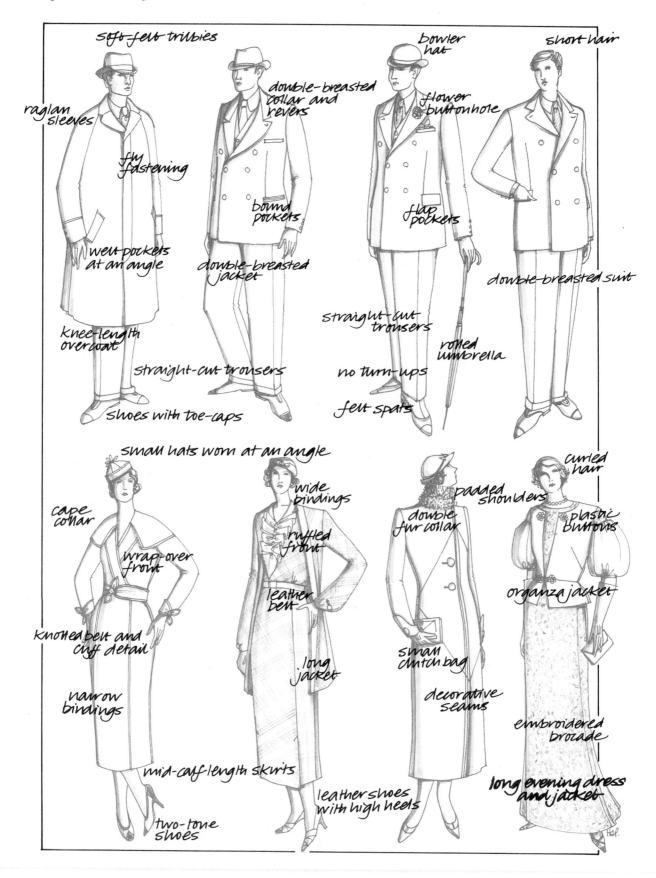

soft-felt trilbies

raglan sleeves

fly fastening

welt pockets at an angle

knee-length overcoat

straight-cut trousers

shoes with toe-caps

double-breasted collar and revers

bound pockets

double-breasted jacket

bowler hat

flower buttonhole

flap pockets

straight-cut trousers

no turn-ups

felt spats

rolled umbrella

short hair

double-breasted suit

small hats worn at an angle

cape collar

wrap-over front

knotted belt and cuff detail

narrow bindings

mid-calf-length skirts

two-tone shoes

wide bindings

ruffled front

leather belt

long jacket

leather shoes with high heels

padded shoulders

double fur collar

small clutch bag

decorative seams

curled hair

plastic buttons

organza jacket

embroidered brocade

long evening dress and jacket

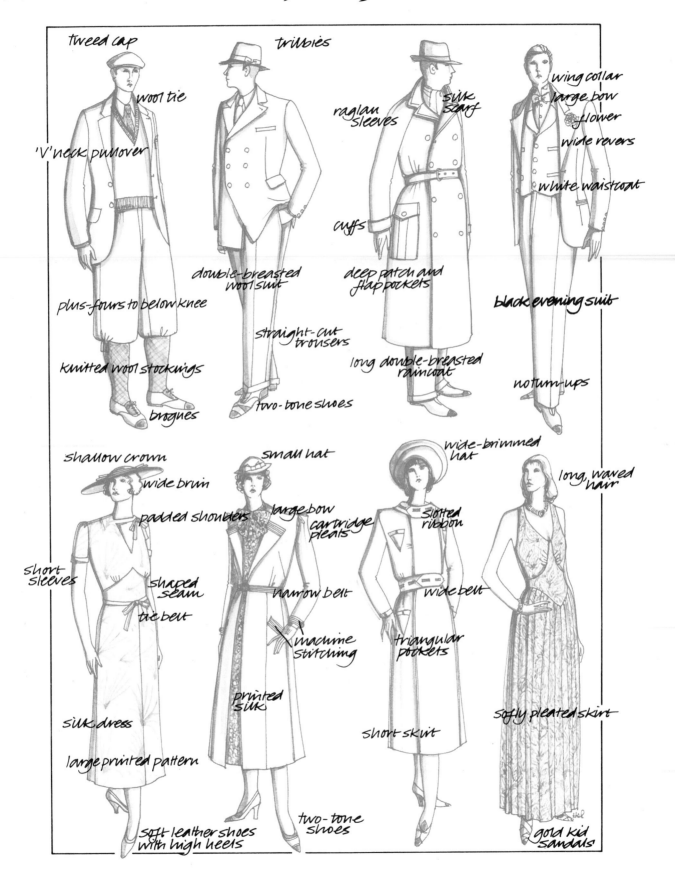

tweed cap

trilbies

wool tie

raglan sleeves

silk scarf

wing collar

large bow

flower

wide revers

'V'neck pullover

white waistcoat

plus-fours to below knee

double-breasted wool suit

deep patch and flap pockets

black evening suit

cuffs

straight-cut trousers

knitted wool stockings

long double-breasted raincoat

no turn-ups

brogues

two-tone shoes

shallow crown

wide brim

small hat

wide-brimmed hat

long, waved hair

padded shoulders

large bow

cartridge pleats

slotted ribbon

short sleeves

shaped seam

narrow belt

wide belt

tie belt

machine stitching

triangular pockets

silk dress

printed silk

softly pleated skirt

large printed pattern

short skirt

soft leather shoes with high heels

two-tone shoes

gold kid sandals

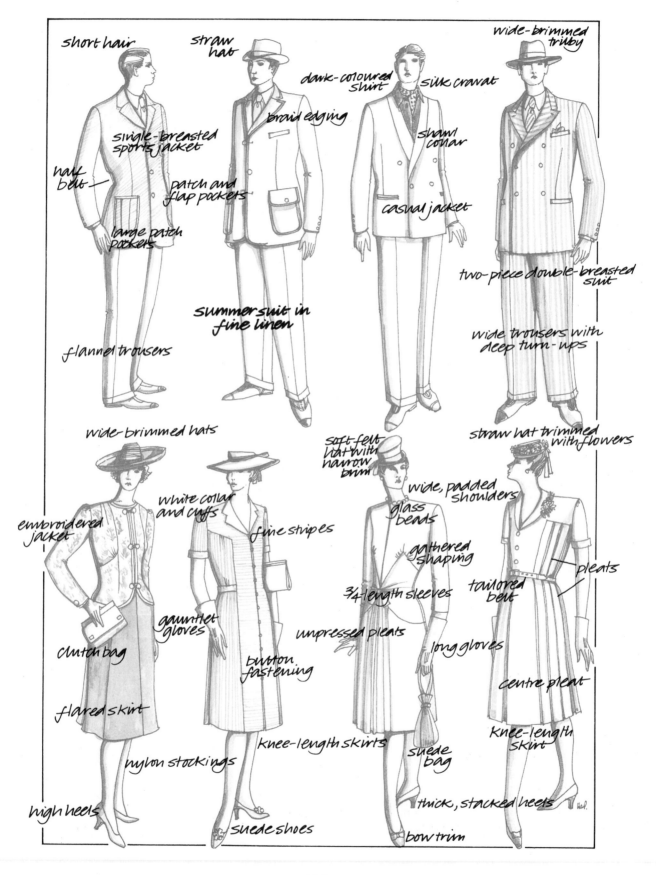

short hair

straw hat

wide-brimmed trilby

dark-coloured shirt

silk cravat

braid edging

single-breasted sports jacket

shawl collar

half belt

patch and flap pockets

casual jacket

large patch pockets

two-piece double-breasted suit

summer suit in fine linen

wide trousers with deep turn-ups

flannel trousers

wide-brimmed hats

soft-felt hat with narrow brim

straw hat trimmed with flowers

wide, padded shoulders

white collar and cuffs

glass beads

fine stripes

embroidered jacket

gathered shaping

pleats

3/4-length sleeves

tailored belt

gauntlet gloves

unpressed pleats

long gloves

clutch bag

button fastening

centre pleat

flared skirt

knee-length skirt

knee-length skirts

suede bag

nylon stockings

high heels

thick, stacked heels

suede shoes

bow trim

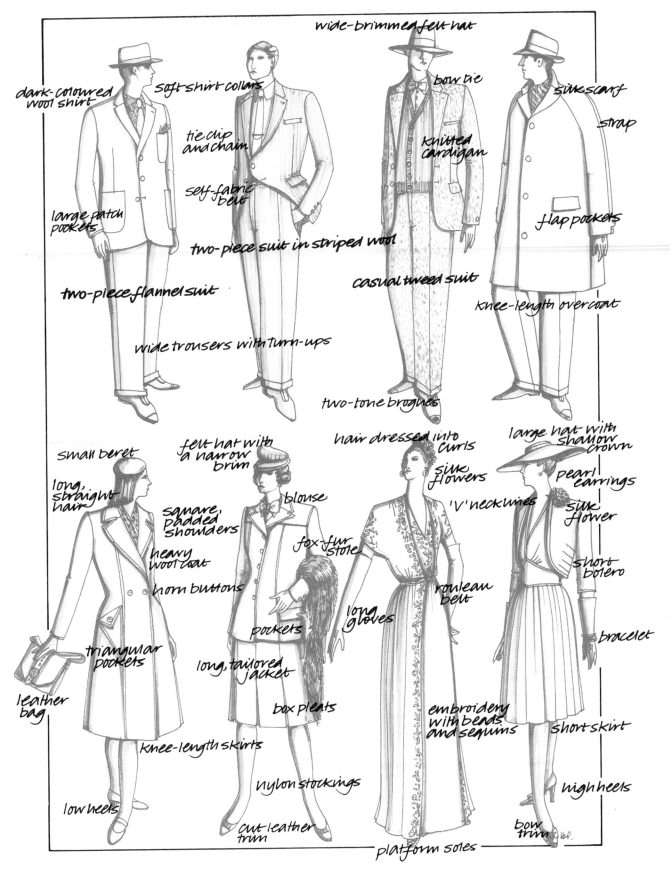

wide-brimmed felt hat

dark-coloured wool shirt

soft shirt collars

bow tie

silk scarf

strap

tie clip and chain

knitted cardigan

self-fabric belt

flap pockets

large patch pockets

two-piece suit in striped wool

casual tweed suit

two-piece flannel suit

knee-length overcoat

wide trousers with turn-ups

two-tone brogues

large hat with shallow crown

small beret

felt hat with a narrow brim

hair dressed into curls

silk flowers

pearl earrings

long, straight hair

square, padded shoulders

blouse

'V' necklines

silk flower

heavy wool coat

fox-fur stole

short bolero

horn buttons

rouleau belt

long gloves

bracelet

triangular pockets

pockets

long, tailored jacket

leather bag

box pleats

embroidery with beads and sequins

short skirt

knee-length skirts

nylon stockings

low heels

high heels

cut-leather trim

bow trim

platform soles

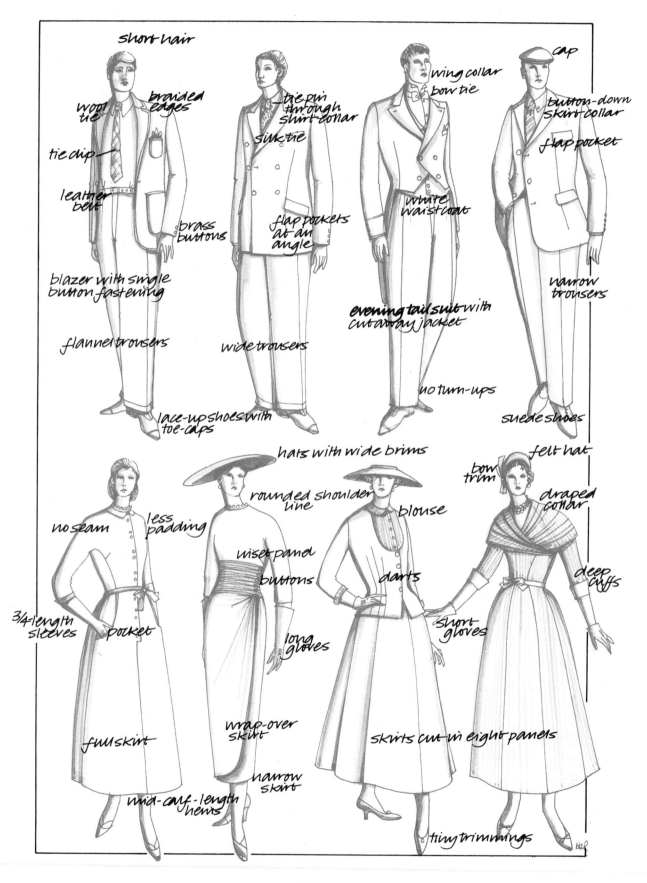

short hair

braided edges

wool tie

tie clip

leather belt

blazer with single button fastening

flannel trousers

brass buttons

lace-up shoes with toe-caps

tie pin through shirt collar

silk tie

flap pockets at an angle

wide trousers

wing collar

bow tie

white waistcoat

evening tail suit with cutaway jacket

no turn-ups

cap

button-down shirt collar

flap pocket

narrow trousers

suede shoes

hats with wide brims

felt hat

bow trim

no seam

less padding

rounded shoulder line

blouse

draped collar

inset panel

buttons

darts

deep cuffs

3/4-length sleeves

pocket

long gloves

short gloves

full skirt

wrap-over skirt

narrow skirt

skirts cut in eight panels

mid-calf-length hems

tiny trimmings

flat cap

hood

machine stitching

wooden toggles

felt trilby

raglan sleeves

cap

velvet bow tie

pleats

long shawl collar

fly fastening

seam

piped pockets

strap and button

welt pocket

patch and flap pockets

knee-length duffle coat

knee-length coats

machine stitching

vent

satin stripe

narrow trousers with turn-ups

no turn-ups

ankle-boots with pointed toes

brogues

curled hair

small pill-box hat

short hair

stiff felt beret

velvet ribbon

blouse

semi-raglan sleeves

graduated beads

organza stole

wide belt

fitted jacket

strapless, boned bodice

short gloves

3/4-length sleeves

narrow skirt

embroidered fabric

3/4-length coat and matching suit

full skirt worn over stiff petticoats

large handbag

shoes with high heels and pointed toes

'ballerina'-length skirt

gold sandals

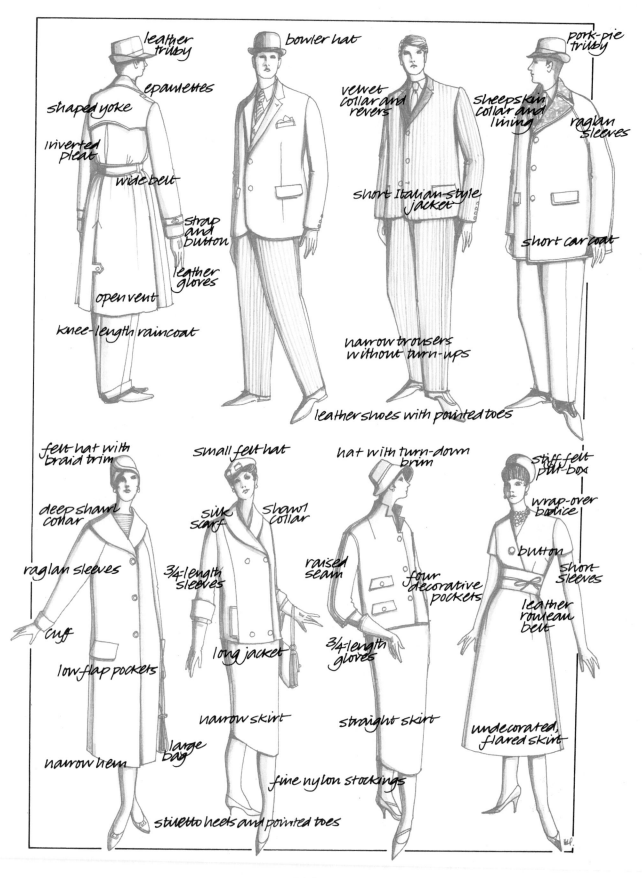

leather trilby

epaulettes

shaped yoke

inverted pleat

wide belt

strap and button

leather gloves

open vent

knee-length raincoat

bowler hat

velvet collar and revers

short Italian-style jacket

narrow trousers without turn-ups

pork-pie trilby

sheepskin collar and lining

raglan sleeves

short car coat

leather shoes with pointed toes

felt hat with braid trim

deep shawl collar

raglan sleeves

cuff

low-flap pockets

narrow hem

small felt hat

silk scarf

shawl collar

3/4-length sleeves

long jacket

narrow skirt

large bag

stiletto heels and pointed toes

hat with turn-down brim

raised seam

four decorative pockets

3/4-length gloves

straight skirt

fine nylon stockings

stiff felt pill-box

wrap-over bodice

button

short sleeves

leather rouleau belt

undecorated, flared skirt

ELIZABETH II · 1952~   (iii) C.1960~63

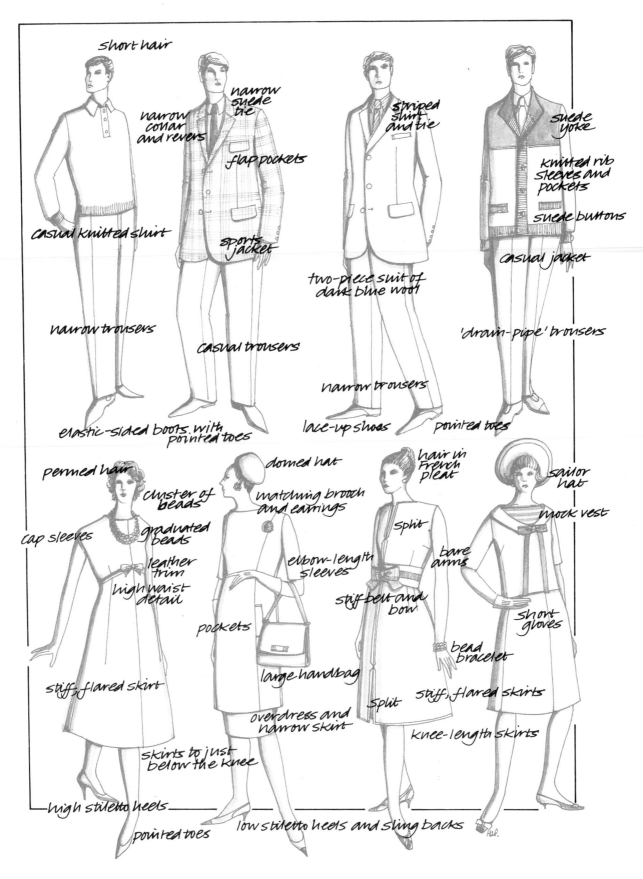

- short hair
- narrow suede tie
- narrow collar and revers
- striped shirt and tie
- suede yoke
- flap pockets
- knitted rib sleeves and pockets
- casual knitted shirt
- sports jacket
- suede buttons
- casual jacket
- two-piece suit of dark blue wool
- narrow trousers
- 'drain-pipe' trousers
- casual trousers
- narrow trousers
- elastic-sided boots with pointed toes
- lace-up shoes
- pointed toes

- permed hair
- domed hat
- hair in French pleat
- sailor hat
- cluster of beads
- matching brooch and earrings
- split
- mock vest
- cap sleeves
- graduated beads
- elbow-length sleeves
- bare arms
- leather trim
- high waist detail
- stiff belt and bow
- short gloves
- pockets
- bead bracelet
- stiff, flared skirt
- large handbag
- stiff, flared skirts
- split
- overdress and narrow skirt
- knee-length skirts
- skirts to just below the knee
- high stiletto heels
- pointed toes
- low stiletto heels and sling backs

125

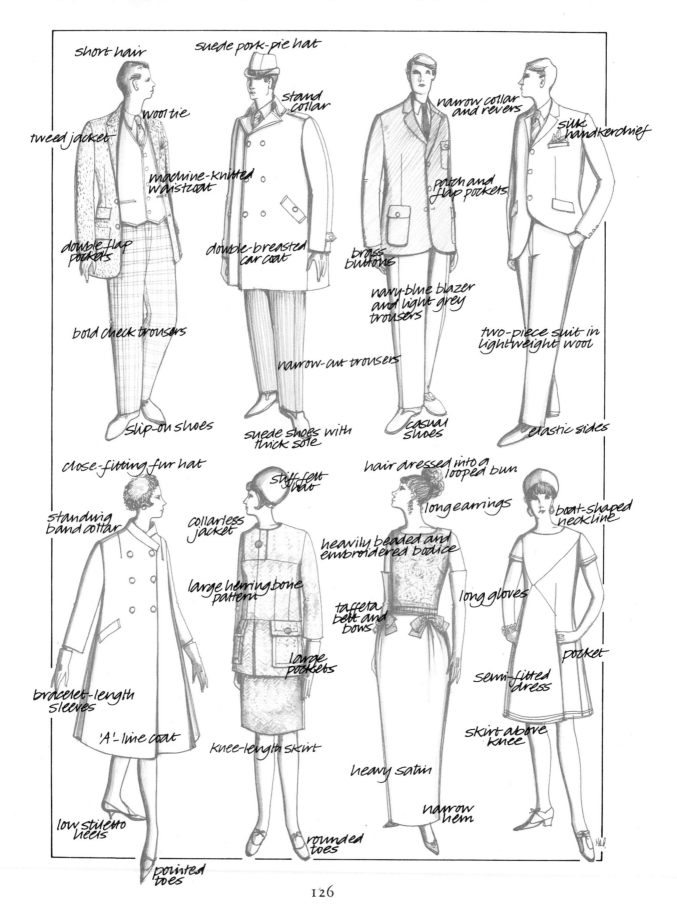

short hair

suede pork-pie hat

wool tie

tweed jacket

stand collar

narrow collar and revers

silk handkerchief

machine-knitted waistcoat

patch and flap pockets

double flap pockets

double-breasted car coat

brass buttons

navy-blue blazer and light grey trousers

two-piece suit in lightweight wool

bold check trousers

narrow-cut trousers

slip-on shoes

suede shoes with thick sole

casual shoes

elastic sides

close-fitting fur hat

stiff felt hat

hair dressed into a looped bun

long earrings

boat-shaped neckline

standing band collar

collarless jacket

heavily beaded and embroidered bodice

long gloves

bracelet-length sleeves

large herringbone pattern

taffeta belt and bows

pocket

large pockets

semi-fitted dress

'A'-line coat

knee-length skirt

skirt above knee

low stiletto heels

heavy satin

narrow hem

rounded toes

pointed toes

Further Reading

Anderson Black, J., and Madge Garland, *A History of Fashion*, Orbis, London, 1975.
A history of dress from the ancient world to the 1970s. Illustrations mostly in colour, with some line drawings. Detailed and informative text.

Arnold, Janet, *Patterns of Fashion*, Macmillan, London, 1964.
Detailed drawings and patterns of women's costumes from 1660 to 1860, taken from original specimens, with full written explanation.

Bentley, Nicolas, *Edwardian Album*, Cardinal, London, 1974.
Photographs of everyday life in the Edwardian era.

Blum, Stella, *Victorian Fashions and Costumes*, Dover, New York, 1974.
Women's costumes, hats, underwear and accessories from *Harper's Bazaar*, 1867–98. Very detailed.

Boucher, François, *A History of Costume in the West*, Thames and Hudson, London, 1965.
From prehistory to the early 1960s. Very detailed text and hundreds of illustrations.

Bradfield, Nancy, *Historical Costumes of England*, Harrap, London, 1958.
Clothes of men and women from 1066 to 1956. Clearly illustrated, with a brief written survey.
——, *Costume in Detail*, Harrap, London, 1968.
Very detailed drawings showing construction, fabric detail, embroidery, etc. Concise text.

Brook, Iris, *A History of English Costume*, Methuen, London, 1937.
A small handbook with many line drawings and a full text.

Bruhn, Wolfgang, and Max Tilke, *A Pictorial History of Costume*, Zwemmer, London, 1955.
A survey of costume from antiquity to the nineteenth century. Brief text with hundreds of drawings, some in colour.

Buckley, V. C., *Good Times*, Thames and Hudson, London, 1979.
Photographs of life between the two World Wars.

Byrne, Penelope, *The Male Image*, Batsford, London, 1979.
General survey of English male fashion. Full, illustrated text.

Clayton Calthrop, Dion, *English Costume*, A. & C. Black, London, 1907.
Text, with illustrations, dealing with the period 1066 to 1830.

Coleridge, Lady Georgina, *The Lady's Realm*, Arrow Books, London, 1972.
A selection from this monthly magazine between November 1904 and April 1905.

Contini, Mila, *Fashion*, Hamlyn, London, 1965.
Illustrated survey from Ancient Egypt to the present.

Cunnington, C. W. and P., the 'Handbook of English Costume' series, Faber and Faber, London, 1952–59.
Indispensable work in five volumes, covering the subject from the Norman Conquest to the nineteenth century. Illustrated.

Cunnington, C. W. and P., and Charles Beard, *A Dictionary of English Costume*, A. & C. Black, London, 1960.
Concise descriptions with line illustrations.

Cunnington, Phillis, *Costume of Household Servants*, A. & C. Black, London, 1974.
Photographs and line drawings showing clothes worn from the Middle Ages to 1900.

Cunnington, Phillis, and Catherine Lucas, *Occupational Costume in England*, A. & C. Black, London, 1967.
Detailed description of working clothes from the eleventh century onwards.

Dorner, Jane, *Fashion in the Twenties and Thirties*, Allan, London, 1973.
——, *Fashion in the Forties and Fifties*, Allan, London, 1975.
Surveys using contemporary photographs.

Fowler, Kenneth, *The Age of the Plantagenet and Valois*, Ferndale, London, 1967.
Detailed illustrated history between 1328 and 1498.

Gaunt, William, *Court Painting in England*, Constable, London, 1980.
Court painting from the Tudors to Victoria.

Gorsline, Douglas, *What People Wore*, Orbis, London, 1978.
Hundreds of drawings, with a brief historical survey.

Hall-Duncan, Nancy, *The History of Fashion Photography*, Alpine, New York, 1979.
Photographs from 1840 to 1970.

Hamilton-Hill, Margot, and Peter A. Bucknell, *The Evolution of Fashion 1066 to 1930*, Batsford, London, 1967.
Detailed drawings of male and female fashions with accompanying patterns and a short text.

Hansen, Henny Harald, *Costume Cavalcade*, Methuen, London, 1954.
Costumes illustrated in colour from Ancient Egypt to 1954.

Harrison, Michael, *The History of the Hat*, Jenkins, London, 1960.
Line drawings and detailed text, covering 4,000 years.

Hartley, Dorothy, *Medieval Costume and Life*, Batsford, London, 1931.
Diagrams, line drawings and some photographs of reconstructed costumes.

Historic Costumes in Pictures, Dover, New York, Constable, London, 1975.
Fashion plates originally published by Braun & Schneider, Munich, 1861–90.

Hopkins, J. C., *The Twentieth Century System of Ladies' Garment Cutting*, Minster, London, 1902.
Detailed instruction in the cutting of women's clothes in the first decade of this century.

Houston, Mary G., *Medieval Costume in England and France*, A. & C. Black, London, 1939.
Clear line drawings of costumes from the thirteenth to the fifteenth century. Full text and some pattern details.

Howell, Georgina, *In Vogue*, Condé Nast, London, 1975.
Drawings and photographs from *Vogue* magazine from 1916 to 1975.

Kelsall, Freda, *How We Used to Live*, MacDonald, London, 1981.
Documentary survey from 1936 to 1953, with contemporary photographs.

Kohler, Carl, *A History of Costume*, Dover, New York, 1928.
Costume and pattern cutting covered in detail from 2,000 BC to the mid nineteenth century. Scholarly and informative text.

Langley-Moore, Doris, *Fashion through Fashion Plates*, Ward Lock, London, 1971.
Fully illustrated, with an informative text, covering the period 1771–1970.

Laver, James, *Costume Through the Ages*, Thames and Hudson, London, 1961.
Easy-to-read line drawings taken from sculpture, painting, etc.
——, *Costume,* Cassell, London, 1963.
Scholarly text with illustrations.
——, *A Concise History of Costume*, Thames and Hudson, London, 1969. (Rev. edn published 1982 as *Costume and Fashion: A Concise History.*)
Well-illustrated general survey.

Lynam, Ruth, *Paris Fashion*, Michael Joseph, London, 1972.
Traces history of couture and some designers. Photographs and drawings. Detailed text.

Polhemus, Ted, and Lynn Procter, *Fashion and Anti-Fashion*, Thames and Hudson, London, 1978.
Different views of what is and is not fashion from various parts of the world.

Pringle, Margaret, *Dance Little Ladies*, Orbis, London, 1977.
Illustrated history of the débutante.

Sansom, William, *Victorian Life in Photographs*, Thames and Hudson, London, 1974.
Scenes from everyday life from the 1860s to 1900.

Scott, Margaret, *Late Gothic Europe 1400–1500*, 'History of Dress' series, Mills and Boon, London, 1980.
Serious text, well illustrated.

Stevenson, Pauline, *Edwardian Fashion*, Allan, London, 1980.
Covers the period 1897 to 1914 in men's and women's fashion, with contemporary illustrations and some modern material.

Strong, Roy, *The English Icon,* Paul Mellon Foundation, London, 1969.
Portrait painting from Elizabeth I to James I. Full, serious text and invaluable illustrations.

Winter, Gordon, *A Country Camera 1844–1914*, Country Life, London, 1966.
——, *A Cockney Camera*, Penguin, London, 1971.
Late nineteenth- and early twentieth-century social history in photographs.
——, *The Golden Years 1903 to 1913*, David & Charles, Newton Abbott, 1975.
A photographic survey.

Yarwood, Doreen, *English Costume*, Batsford, London, 1951.
Costume in detail from the second century BC to 1967. Line drawings and text, covering a full range of detail and accessories.